Working Dogs Beyond the Basics

Handler Training Guide

By Patrick Currey

K9 Operations

This book may be purchased in bulk at special discounted prices for sales promotions, fund raising, corporate gifts or educational purposes. Special editions can also be created to specifications. For details pat@k9operations.com

We will try to accommodate all reasonable requests. Please feel free to discuss your needs with us so that we may have the opportunity to serve you better. For information regarding the authorized use of any of the contents of this document, contact the author directly at 734-532-2013 or visit www.k9operations.com

Book Design: Competitive Edge Group
Manufactured in the United States
Printed by On Demand

ISBN-10: 0989521761
ISBN-13: 978-0-9895217-6-5

TO MY READERS

During my years of working dogs, I can honestly say that I have learned more of what not to do with a dog/program than what to do. Learning from mistakes of others, as well as myself, has taught me to become a better dog handler/trainer and coach.

My mistakes are your agency/company gains.

There are a few mottos I have adopted over the years:

> ➢ When you get three dog people together, the only thing they agree on?...Two agree that one doesn't know what they are talking about.

> ➢ 99% of the time it is the handler's fault. The other 1% of the time...It's the handler's fault.

> ➢ Those that don't know history are destined to repeat it.

To have a successful K9 Program, managers must learn to how to help them become as productive as possible. They have to utilize their resources to the fullest and most importantly successfully train and maintain their assets...the detector dogs.

Anyone Can Train A Dog... Working A Dog Is An "Art"

Working a dog is an art that few truly master and we as humans are not maximizing the dogs true abilities to their fullest capabilities.

Dogs are always telling us a story, its our job to observe, interpret what they are telling us and to effectively correct or reward the behaviors we are seeing.

Simply put; there is much more to a working dog than simply buying a dog and training it. Remember it will be you that will bring the dog to success or make a dog fail.

Today's working dog programs are all destined to fail just as the early programs did; not because the working dog isn't affective, but humans don't recognize history and is destine to repeat itself.

This book is an opinion of a trainer/ handler that has experienced many facets of the k9 industry. It in itself will not make you a better handler, but its goal is to open your brain to see the story that your dog is telling you; hopefully you will be wise enough to listen. History is repeating itself in our working dog programs; if you don't wake up and start expecting more - it too will fail.

If I can assist you in any way, feel free to contact me www.k9operations.com

Pat Currey

CONTENTS
Forward

Forward

Denise Donovan
Founder/Director/Author
International Bed Bug Resource Authority

It's well known that detection dogs have a superior olfactory compared to humans and are extremely valuable in many venues from contraband to corpses and most recently in the medical field.

Because of the cryptic nature of the bed bug and difficulty of finding them, people started training dogs on the scent of live bed bugs and their eggs to assist in locating areas that were infested. One thing though; the ease of entering the industry as a professional handler and team was as simple as writing a check. And equally easy was any obedience trainer or retired canine handler could call themselves a professional handler trainers. This greatly disturbed those who were professionals in the detection dog industry.

People from all walks of life started grabbing up dogs from pounds or anywhere else they could to get them quickly trained up enough to provide them to those who could write a check.

Within a short amount of time people began questioning the qualifications of those who were training and selling these dogs. These dogs were handed over to anyone who could write a check and after a three to five day training given carte blanche as a "professional bed bug handler and team". It's amazing that one would not have to take any type of ethology or even basic obedience courses and no previous education, accredited schooling or degree was required. Do you think a drug, bomb or medical detection handler takes a three day course and are let loose in their perspective industry? Bed bug dogs and handlers are not any less important.

Soon, rumor started flying throughout the pest control industry and dog teams were being accused of "alerting" where there were no bed bugs and in many cases not alert when there were bed bugs. Why you ask?? Because that's the way they were being trained.

These dogs weren't interested in working, had no work ethic, were only interested in whether it was going to get that piece of beef jerky or not and would sit and stare at their handlers food pouches in anticipation of reward. As you will learn in this book, the dog will only do what it is trained to do.

Unfortunately, it is the handlers here that were failing victim. They had no formal training and didn't know how a dog works or how to correct behavior or maintain these dogs. Their intentions were honorable, yet they spent their hard-earned money and were facing scrutiny in the field for not knowing what they were doing wrong.

The industry as a whole sees a need to change this handler behavior; and that is exactly what this book is all about. Pat is a master of his trade, has years of education and accreditations as a handler trainer as well as being a professional handler himself. With this book he steers you past what many call being the "idiot on the other end of the leash" and will show you where you and your team are now and what YOU need to do become a true professional.

Parts of this book may be upsetting to those who have big egos or think they know it all; but alternately as the layers open up a better realization and understanding will come forward for you.

His years of work are insightful and his guidance and help offers lasting results. This book has been written and re-written many time to best educate handlers on the foundations of a working dog, working dog teams and working dog handlers.

Pat has a huge caring heart and wants to help this industry navigate the right course to becoming professionals. He's done one wonderful job putting together this book based on his experience and scientific facts that have been undisputed for over a hundred years and provides you with the tools, education and foundation to move forward in the working dog industry.

Denise Donovan
Founder/Director/Author
International Bed Bug Resource Authority

Patrick Currey

ONE

Expect The Best

Having a working dog can be a very effective tool for humans to utilize. The working dog industry is unregulated for the most part, which leaves the doors wide open for personal opinions and beliefs. Humans must first understand that we do not teach our dogs to find anything; a dog can find anything that has odor if they simply utilize their nose. Essentially what we are teaching our dogs is to utilize their sense of smell for our benefit on command, in a manner for which we feel appropriate.

Reward or Correct

While there may be many opinions and beliefs on the right way to train a dog; there are no trade secrets, there is no **"right"** way and there are only two rules that you must follow. **You either reward behavior or you correct behavior**. This is not my belief, this is scientific fact.

Topics of much argument such as the best breed for working, pedigree vs. mutt, the best way to reward, male/female, accuracy, ability, how long can they work, effectiveness; are all arbitrary if we don't stick to the facts for which science has proven unequivocally. This simply means one has to set aside personal beliefs and strictly train based on facts that are being presented by the dog.

The two main ingredients of successful working dogs are drive and recoverability.

The dog you choose for your program should fit your needs but ultimately drive is the most important value your dog must possess in order to do this work; equally important is the ability for your dog to recover from a given situation. There are so many variables when it comes to communicating exactly what we want our dogs to do for us.

Success and failure will always fall upon the shoulders of the handler, for it is they who are continually communicating and interpreting their behaviors.

Regardless of your beliefs the two basic rules will always be there; either **Reward or Correct** behavior.

Shaping behavior in a dog isn't difficult if they have the right drive within them. Shaping behavior simply means any natural behavior of the dog translated into a task upon your command; if done properly can be achieved in a very short timeframe. Once the dog knows the task in its basic format, you are simply teaching work ethic.

A dog is always going to be a dog. It is a social creature and will have the same shortcomings that we as humans have. Remember, we studied dogs to teach us about human behavior; Ian Pavlov wrote the first dog training book and laid out all the rules from which you must abide or the results will be undesirable.

Human interaction is where the problems lie; we want one thing and communicate another.

Human expectations also shape our dogs behavior. Much of your dog's humanistic behavior has to do with how we behave toward them. High expectations that a handler has of themselves can be communicated down to the dog. A handler communicates their expectations, as well as their credibility as a leader as seen by the dog, and demonstrates daily what and how things need to be done. Both good and bad behaviors are taught to the dog; unfortunately more bad behaviors are inadvertently taught and are topics of many discussions, finger pointing and generally blaming the dog.

Leadership

Leadership has become cliché in the dog industry as the action of leading or "communicating properly" may be achieved in your head, but not necessarily from your dog's point of view. A good leader can bring out the best in anyone or anything, including the dog.

As a handler you need to bolsters the dog's self-confidence, making it possible for him to achieve more than he may have initially believed possible. A dog knows little of human law and will revert directly to dog law.

We live our lives in a social format under "Human Law". Dog's also live their lives in a social format which is very similar to humans with a few major differences.

We will go into further detail of these rules and what the laws are later in the book, however it is important for you to understand the importance of similar, but different laws.

The handler's expectations of their dog have their strongest and most powerful influence in times of uncertainty and turbulence in which your dog will look to you for the answers.

A true handler expects the best and will always make decisions which will benefit the training, by communicating to the dog in a format to which it will understand.

Walk before you run, as reaching greatness takes a lot of time, quality training and patience. You may have a high then a low in the same day, or even same training program, so you must learn to deal with these properly and how to communicate them effectively.

Remember your dog is always telling you a story, it is your job to observe, interpret what they are telling you and effectively correct or reward the behaviors you are seeing. This is no easy task and will become frustrating; so remember it will be you that will bring the dog to success or make a dog fail.

Patrick Currey

TWO

The Working Dog

Working dogs have been utilized for many years in our great country. It is important to know about history as it is destine to repeat itself.

As early as 1907, Law enforcement was the earliest recorded uses of a working dog in the United States. From March 1907 when the South Orange police started America's first police patrol dog program through 1952; only 14 all-purpose patrol dog-handler programs are known to have been implemented in America police forces. In 1940 the cost for a fully trained dog was quite substantial at around $1000. Incidentals such as dog food, veterinarian care and training averaged about $80 per month; these cost aren't much different in today's dollar.

The main use of the dog was for protection aspects of law enforcement and what we consider today a "**single purpose**" working dog. While the dog served the departments effectively there were many pitfalls that cause the programs to fail individually and collectively.

Today we are seeing essentially the same reasons for our working dog programs to fail as they did in the first programs of our country. The initial investment, training and maintaining expenses, unable to maintain proficiency, the dogs tended to be nervous and excitable and generally worked for one handler. Some were vicious and attacked other officers or members of the handlers family. The training and conditioning of the dog also interfered with the officers essential police duties.

The handlers were not K9 specialist, rather officers first with assigned duties as a dog handler. This tasked the department's budget as funding to organize and operate a specialty unit were not available.

In short, it was inevitable that the advantages of a working dog program were outweighed by the never ending cost of them.

Budgets were not the only reason the working dog programs failed. The working dog handler led to its demise. Handlers left the force or became disinterested and/or promoted and became unable to continue as a K9 specialist. Administrators also became frustrated with the insufficient quality of dogs, local politics, and handlers laxness.

Many of the dogs utilize were well unsuited for police work. Yet the consequences of dog bites, lack of special vehicles needed for the working dogs, administrators not learning how to properly utilize their working dog team; all led to the demise of the early working dog programs.

World War II also depleted our countries working dogs in the call for all dogs to join America's fight. After World War II the decline of the working dog program in our country as a whole became almost non-existent. There were small working dog programs during the Korean War and we saw a large use of working dogs during the Vietnamese War. In that time our local law enforcement didn't help the working dog program gain success during the race riots of the 60s and 70s.

During the 1980s a resurgence of the working dog program as a whole group grew by leaps and bounds. With the war on drugs came great revenue for many police departments in the utilization of dogs for narcotics detection which became a valuable tool. Our militaries working dog program was also gaining success and today is a large program of any country.

With the war on drugs becoming the popular fight; the working dog industry as a whole group grew by leaps and bounds. Many of the programs were funded by government grants or local groups. With the new need for an abundance of narcotics detection dogs, a new industry was started throughout the country.

This new industry was essentially unregulated as there were virtually no laws or regulations governing the program. There were only a few training centers devoted to the instruction of working dog handlers and training of working dogs. Many of these programs turned to the local civilian trainers who had experience in obedience, tracking, and personal protection; but for the most part no detection experience.

Following the rise of the detection dog program during this decade, many court rulings and laws establishing governing of the reliability, effectiveness and use the detection dog became law. Vast majorities of these laws started at the federal level, but significant numbers also came from local disparities. These laws not only governed the detection portion of the working dog program but also the dogs ability to find humans and it's use of force to protect the handlers.

These laws outlined certification standards, record-keeping and mandated training. This also created the now experienced police officers beginning training centers on their own and essentially taking the working dog out of the civilian dog industry.

While the experience and street credentials of these officers gave them an easy avenue to capitalize on the police dog training market; many conflicts also caused the decrease reliability of their programs.

There have been many attempts to regulate training standards outside of the federally mandated weekly training requirements. However, there are still no regulations for who can become a K9 trainer, course outlines or basic requirements for that of the working dog or the initial training of the working dog handler.

Many of these programs became nonexistent, as the reliability of the detection dogs were in question by fellow officers and administrators. Handlers laziness, jealousy, egos and overall effectiveness; as well as legal issues and the drop in the economy creating budgeting issues rose once again. The surge of the working dog program in North America became an amenity many could not afford.

War always creates jobs and after 9/11 our country saw the greatest increase of working dogs throughout our military, civilian contractors and local law enforcement agencies. Our main focus shifted from narcotics interdiction to explosive detection dogs. This created much controversy within the working dog industry as many felt there was a difference in certification and training of an explosive detection dog vs. a narcotics detection dog.

The uses of civilian programs also increased as many hospitals and other large venues felt it was important to have their own explosive detection K9 teams. With this surge of working dog teams and the continued bickering back and forth many new certification authorities increased.

As the history of the working dog program has been very consistent in its increase and decline; within 10 years many of the explosive detection teams decreased with an estimated number of 50 to 60%. These programs were depleted due to our economy and a false sense of security as the war on terror began to wind down.

Over the past 10 to 15 years there is been an increase in the usage of working dogs in the civilian market especially in the pest-control industry. A properly trained detection dog can effectively and reliably detect unwanted pests such as bed bugs, termites, moles and much more. The use of a working dog for pest-control can be utilized much like an explosive detection dog would be utilized for the security of a building is searching.

Checks And Balances

Regardless of what a working dog is being utilized for, be it military, local law enforcement, pest control, medical or civilian markets; a working dog is only good if there is an established canine program to support it. The canine program is essentially an internal checks and balances to ensure those that they serve are getting highest-quality working dog team possible.

Working dog and federal programs such as our military, US customs and border protection and other federal law enforcement K9 Teams, all have a program that regulates the procurement of their working dogs, the hiring of their handlers, the training center for which both K9 and handlers are trained, the duration of training and education to which both dog and handler receive.

It also includes usage of the working dog in the field, training both daily and weekly, training records, certification standards, training material, training environments, veterinarian care, boarding and much, much more.

Simply put; there is much more to a working dog than simply buying a dog and training it.

These standards have allowed the working dogs of our nation to increase and grow stronger each year. On the contrary these standards have not trickled into the civilian working dog industry, to include law enforcement entities and the pest-control industry. There are no standards for the working dog, the training centers, the trainers, the education of the handlers or even standards established for maintenance training of these teams. The pest-control industry national standards for training a working dog team for bed bug detection is only four days.

Patrick Currey

THREE

Principles Of Dog Training

Working a dog is an art form. There is much more to working a dog then telling commands and far more important for the handler to have an education on "why" before they learn "how".

"Art Form" - Human effort to imitate, supplement, alter, or counteract the work of nature, a trade or craft that applies such a system of principles and methods, Skill that is attained by study, practice, or observation.

Learning to work a dog takes time and patience. You're working dog should be thought of like a professional athlete and should also be worked and trained like one. Each athlete starts out at a very basic level to learn their craft. A handler will also have different levels of duties as well as be the teacher and coach of the dog.

Regardless of who is training the dog, the type of work or the type of dog, all training follows the same principles based on scientific fact. Essentially, Pavlov wrote the first dog training book and his discoveries are what we base all of our dogs training from. It is often forgotten by humans that we actually studied animals to understand our own social structure.

Psychologists are learning more about how we learn every day and will continue to do so for decades to come. Without attempting to propound a definition, it can easily be said that dogs have now been studied so thoroughly that there are tools and methods to influence behavior profoundly and in a fraction of the time it formerly took to accomplish the same results.

A dog's is always telling you a story, just because you are able to understand or interpret the story they are nonetheless telling a story.

This will be a very humbling experience for most, however you expect to achieve greatness, you must be able to look at every angle not just an opinion.

Each handler influences the dog to behave the way he has been taught, this does not always mean good behavior and more often not mean bad behavior. Inadvertently you are always shaping your dog's behavior. They are learning both good and bad from us and you as a handler are the sole reason the dog succeeds or fails. It is most worthwhile to understand certain psychological principles, even though learning about them may require considerable study.

It is very important for you to understand the basic principles of dog training. These principles were learned many years ago by studying dogs, rats and other animals in order to learn human behavior. Unfortunately humans determine which of these principles they want to follow and which they choose not to, thus a conflict in the industry.

Ian Pavlov discovered the very principles by which every social creature to include our dog follows. B.F. Skinner expounded on the positives and negatives of social structure. Many studies conducted by other great minds throughout the world have utilized animals to make their point. As a handler it is very important for you to obey these simple principles, but will be very hard for you to achieve.

In a nutshell, what Pavlov discovered from studying dogs put in simple terms is as follows:

"Any stimulus an organism can perceive is capable of eliciting any reaction the organism is capable of making. This means that virtually any sound, sight, or smell, can influence the way our muscles tense or relax, our moods fluctuate, or even the way our attitudes are formed"

To break it down for you as a handler, any stimulus your dog can perceive can be actions which equal a valued reward.

To quantify it for you, your dog has an ability to perceive the slightest changes of your body, your tone, and your smell as a reward or correction.

Just because you as a handler feel you are correct with your dog in the way you look, you sound or the way you smell, can contradict what you feel. The same goes for rewarding your dog; just because you feel like you're rewarding the dog doesn't mean you're rewarding it.

A reward is only a reward if it is rewarding, and a correction is only a correction if it corrects. Not rewarding can be correcting and not correcting can be rewarding. This is based off of the two rules of dog training; "you either reward behavior or you correct behavior". While this may seem very complicated it is actually very simple and must be applied to every aspect of what you get your dog to do from how it sits, sleeps, eats and most importantly works.

These basic fundamentals are also influenced genetically. This is not to say that genetics alter the rules, but just like with humans some are better at understanding and following than others. Regardless of the pedigree, the breed, the gender, or where the dog is from; it is first and foremost a dog.

Dogs operate under dog law which is very similar but very different from human law. What is not socially acceptable in human law is the crotch of another human, however in dog law this is a very socially acceptable trait. You as a human have to understand you cannot take the dog out of the dog, it will always be a dog. Not all dogs are created equal and not all dogs have the desire or ability to be working dogs, no different than every human having ability to become a doctor or professional athlete.

The drive in a working dog is the first and most important aspect of training; the ability for the dog to recover is equally important. Drive is the natural ability for the dog to value a reward to please the rewarder. Essentially the dog has to be able to work in any venue and must maintain their desire to work for that reward no matter what; not all dogs have this ability.

Stress is inevitable, if your dog cannot recover from a stressful event from something scary or something distracting, no matter how much drive the dog has, it will not be able to work.

FOUR

The Dog's Mind

One of the big problems that I have noticed in the K9 world is that most training is conducted with the human in mind, when the simplistic method would be to work a dog as a dog. It is funny that most kenneled hunting dogs don't have the issues that working dogs do. While that may sound goofy to you, if you think about the fact that a dog will act differently with a pack of other dogs, than with a pack of humans. Why is that? Simply, because dogs speak dog, not human, then us smart humans try to treat and work our dogs like humans, with dog abilities.

We will first look at the mind of the dog, which is basically what your job as a handler will be to learn to understand what your dog is trying to tell you. Know that a dog is always communicating something both in and out.

Your job as a handler is to interpret what your dog is telling you and communicate back to them if they are conducting a good or bad behavior.

It must also be noted that your dog is a patterned animal, their evil mathematicians can and will find the most unlikely patterns in what you may perceive as a pattern less event.

Is very important for you as a handler to understand communication, and how our communication differs from the dogs. It doesn't matter what you think matters or what the dog perceives and the dog has the ability to perceive from more venues then we as humans are attuned to.

Many people overlook the most simplistic of communications, but be assured your dog will not miss any of them. If your dog truly has the ability to be working dog, the only reason they shouldn't succeed is because you failed to communicate properly to your dog.

Bad Behavior vs. Good Behavior?

One has to first clarify good and bad behavior. This is often overlooked by humans as they actually treat their dogs like a human. When in retrospect most humans allow their dog to treat them in a manner that they would never take from a human being.

If you were to take and write a list of everything that you don't like about a human you are close with, and ask yourself would I be friends with this person if I saw this list before I knew them? The same goes for your dog, if you are to write all the bad behaviors your dog has an down on paper would you want this dog in your home if it wasn't already in your family?

Bad behavior - Any behavior you don't like.

Being afraid, aggressive, playful, jumping, chewing, sitting, standing; the list is limitless. You also have to expound on this as a working handler, as there are so many different applications for this mindset. If your dog is sitting improperly, not healing and the list goes on. Any behavior you don't like is a bad behavior!

Good behavior - Any behavior you do like.

Being afraid, aggressive, playful, jumping, chewing, sitting, standing; again the list is limitless. I know I listed the same above; the point is if you like it either way it is a good behavior. As a working dog handler we must always work towards perfection and it takes time, repetition, and patients in order to teach the dog exactly how we want them to perform a task. When they are doing the behavior you want you need a bridge word that will tell them they are performing the behavior in the way you want.

Correction and Reward?

Correction - Is a correction if it corrects.

Corrections have to correct to be a correction; this means your dog has to believe it is being corrected and the correction has to stop the behavior for it to be an actual correction.

Reward - Is anything that rewards. Reward isn't a reward unless it is rewarding; this means your dog has to believe it is being rewarded for the behavior.

Note - Not all corrections have to be physical and not all rewards are monetary.

A correction can be done inadvertently for a good behavior and a reward can be done for a bad behavior. If you don't correct a behavior like jumping or fear, you are automatically rewarding it. More behaviors are shaped inadvertently. Two key factors you must always ask- What am I doing to reward and what am I doing to correct said behavior?

Remember, there are only two rules in dog training. You reward behavior or you correct behavior. You are taking a social creature that has a very powerful nose in trying to teach it to work for you in environments that aren't natural for them.

If you don't ingrain these two rules in your everyday lifestyle with your dog, you will find your dog is very frustrated, confused and will eventually just do what it "feels you wanted" it to do instead of "what it is rewarded for and knows to do".

The most minor corrections like a simple tug on the leash can be enough to correct a good behavior.

For example: you're walking with your dog to work from point A to point B. In your mind you need to get to point B to start working, however in between your dog smells the odor in which you taught them to find, but you're focused on going to point B give the dog a small tug on the leash, therefore *correcting a good behavior*; it's that simple.

How Dogs Communicate

Scent- All creatures use scent for communication, with the exception of humans. This doesn't mean we can't smell, just that we don't use it as communication. Scent is a **LANGUAGE** that goes in and out of your dog.

This means they communicate outwardly with odor to all creatures (to humans); to include taking odor in (from humans).

Each odor simply has a positive or negative effect on your dog. Some is engrained into their evolutionary DNA, the rest is learned socially. The key here is that humans can't smell odor from the dog's communication, but the dog does understand your odors.

Humans produce odor for which the dog does have the ability to smell. You have chemical changes in your body for every emotion and body function that the dog understands.

Happy, sad, glad, mad, cancer, pregnant, weak, strong, etc… all have odors the dog can identify. You communicate to your dog through odor and have no control over it. We can't smell the scent, but we can see it if you know what to look for.

Body Language

For every odor your dog produces, both in and out, there is a body language to go with it. Your goal is to observe and piece together what the behavior changes equal. They are there, just not always prevalent if you're not looking or putting it together with the behavior.

Not all body languages equal what we have been told. For example: a tail wag does not equal happy any more than a smile means I am happy. Think of body language as an **Action** that needs an equal or opposite action to reward or correct the behavior of.

Reaction happens after the behavior is underway or completed and all too often humans react to behaviors they should act upon; how unwanted behavior can get started. **Totality** also plays a big role in the body language with the action you must have.

For example: Knowing your dog is scared of an object, your action would be to keep the leash tight to prevent the dog from running away and the totality of the situation (scary versus playful) determines the action you take. Reaction of the same scenario is to allow the dog to run away, thus rewarding the behavior.

Tone

Humans biggest form of communication; "It's not what you say, it's how you say it". Dogs do understand and learn our tones very quickly. Even though the science is there (Pavlov, Skinner, etc...), we often misuse our tone with animals. Just remember Pavlov used tone to shape behavior in his dog.

One of the biggest advantages you can have with any dog; establish your tone(s) from the most positive to the least negative to what they equal. While our dog(s) don't utilize tone the way we do, it doesn't mean they can't learn ours. Utilize tone as a marker to establish a behavior; a negative tone for a bad behavior and a positive for a good behavior. **Tone** must also be paired with a **Touch** to establish its meaning and most importantly with consistency.

You can't say **NO** or **GOOD** in the right tone over and over again (like most people say "Sit" to a dog). Say it, pause for a moment to allow the dog the opportunity to do the proper behavior, then correct or reward accordingly.

When establishing a tone with the behavior, it is important to physically say the word in conjunction with the action. Saying "**Sit**" while placing the dog in a sitting position, **No** while correcting the dog and **Good** while rewarding the dog.

Consistency and timing is the key, paired with the totality of the situation. Remember a bad behavior is one you don't like, but if you don't correct or use a "**Tone Marker**" at the appropriate time, the dog will not understand what they are being rewarded or corrected for.

Start out having fun with the dog, play "**Tone Games**". Have a treat and make a kissing noise to draw the dog's attention. When they approach, say Good in a mild happy tone, then give a treat. If the dog doesn't comply, a light **NO** tone; then make the dog comply (bring them to you), repeat **Good** in a lesser tone (proper tone for appropriate action), followed with the reward (treat).

Utilize your **TONE** always and often and as a marker to teach our dog when shaping behavior. Constantly saying the word (Sit, Sit, Sit, Sit, Sit) is not proper utilization of your tone. This would mean No, No, No, No, No or Good, Good, Good, Good, Good are not correct either; unless an appropriate action follows each tone word (the dog goes from one behavior to another).

As a human we use a tone scale in our communication values. How you say the word "NO" has different meanings based on the tone value that you utilize. If you think of it on a scale from 1-10 = the most passive way to say something, 0 = Neutral and 11-20 the most aggressive way to say something. According to this a #3 -"No" has a different meaning of a #15 "No" and a #7 "Good" has a different meaning than a #19 "Good".

No - Wrong. Not always will a correction follow, but will if the behavior continues. Must be utilized at the moment any behavior you want to correct and in the tone according to the severity of the negative action.

Good - Right. Not always will a reward follow, but may depending on the behavior. Must be utilized at the moment of any behavior you want to reward and it the tone appropriate for the behavior.

OK - Free or Release. Depending on the training, may have a monetary reward.

Done - Done and Will have a correction if the behavior does not stop. Also in the same category Out, Off, Leave-it, Quiet, Stop has the same meaning

Relax is also utilized the opposite of done as it doesn't include a correction but a touch that will calm them down.

Example: When teaching an established dog sit, down to a stand (starting in a stand).

With a 4-5 Tone the command - **Sit** (dog doesn't), **No** (6-8 Tone to mark the wrong behavior), the dog sits = **Good** (1-3 tone, because the dog didn't on the first command), **Down** (the dog does properly)

Good (5-6 tone), **Stand** (the dog does properly) followed immediately with an **OK** followed by the reward (rewarding the behavior you want taught). O.K. must be said prior to going for the reward, to ensure the dog doesn't associate the action with the reward.

It will take some time for you to make this a muscle memory, but the dog will get it far faster than you if you are consistently utilizing the right tone for the totality of the situation. Properly utilizing tone is the hardest thing for a handler to achieve. Learning and utilizing tone words are going to be much harder and far more important to your training than you will ever imagine.

It will be very hard for you to become versed in the application, timing and tone of them, but when you get it right communication will improve and you will be working as a team.

Touch

The most controversial form of communication and the simplest to explain. Touch is either a positive or a negative (+/-), you either correct or reward. It isn't a correction if it doesn't correct or a reward if it doesn't reward.

Most often the inappropriate touch is given by humans. Humans may think they are correcting when they are rewarding. The dog continues to play when you are correcting, does not constitute a correction. The dog is frightened and you pamper it, thus reinforcing being afraid.

The simplest way to explain this:

Corrections and rewards have to be a foundation, not a rule. Teach the dog your foundation (your rules), ensure they know them in every environment and correct or reward for the totality of the situation.

Example One: Dog playing tug or ball. **Out** (5-6 tone) dog doesn't. **No, Out** (dog is still playing). If you continue to tug in efforts to regain the reward, the dog will see this as part of the game, thus tug more.

After the second **NO**, simply pull the dog's nose to your leg or hold the collar so they can't keep tugging until they let go. **OK** (3-4 tone) let the dog tug as soon as they let go and **O.K.** is said to reward letting go (establishes a reward for letting go of something they enjoy). **Out** (seconds after the tug game, because you don't want to reward the fact the dog didn't let go on the first out), Dog releases quickly = **O.K.** and a big tug game to show the difference for releasing the first time commanded.

Out the dog when finished followed by **Done**. The dog releases the tug, Done. If the dog attempts to grab the tug, correct. Don't play a game, leave the tug for the dog to grab or not. If the dog grabs, correct; if not a simple **Good** will suffice.

Example Two: Something scares the dog and you coddle it, telling it softly it will be o.k. this reinforces the fear. Simple **Relax** in a matter of fact tone, followed by some aggressive rubbing and patting (like if you were patting someone on the back) can mean bring the dog out of the fear. Make them stay and address the fear (if possible), but never let them avoid it because they are scared.

Communication is the backbone of every relationship and failure to communicate properly is a demise of the same relationships. It is paramount as a handler to effectively communicate to your dog at all times and more importantly understand your dog's communication to you. This can't be affected by personal beliefs as it often does in the K9 industry. More often than not we are inadvertently rewarding more bad behaviors that we are teaching good behaviors.

FIVE

The Effects Of Genetics And Breeding

There is great controversy in the K9 Industry on what dog makes the best working dog. Humans put way to much stock in pedigrees, breeds and looks. Every dog has the basic abilities to be a working dog, but Not every dog can be a working dog.

Genetic manipulation has virtually no effect on behavior as you cannot produce dogs that can unlock kitchen doors. Breeding selectively can produce dogs that herd better or are more prone to retrieve as well as other desirable traits that benefit our working and domestic needs.

Through genetics behavior can be influence but no more than that. Just because the father is a champion and the mother is a champion doesn't mean that their offspring will be champions. There are many other facets such as social structure and proper training may have strengthened weaker genetic traits.

No matter who the parents are of the dogs both the good traits and the bad traits get spilt between all the dogs. This means that one puppy may have stronger or weaker traits, one can have all the good, one all the bad.

Selective breeding does help if done properly. For example Michael Jordan marrying Serena Williams and having nine children. Both are very successful athletes, strong drive, too good-looking. This does not mean all nine children will have the exact same abilities that they had individually or collectively. One, two or even three of the children may have the same attributes as their parents, but because they can have the same social drive their success can be limited.

Three of the kids may be very athletic, through to be very good-looking and three may have it all, but that doesn't mean that any of them will have the same success with their parents have. Socially each of the kids will be different individually, taking praise and correction differently as well as the general outlook on life.

They are born with every trait they will ever have, you can influence them socially but you cannot stop what was started at birth. An alcoholic has a gene that was inside of them at birth, it may never turn on that person may never become an alcoholic no matter what social trauma they faced. However, once the genes turned on you can never turn it off again.

We see this in our dogs all the time. Just because a dog is a German Shepherd doesn't make it a police dog, just because the dog is a black lab doesn't mean it can swim. Dogs that are born with the chicken little gene may be able to overcome its innate need to be scared through proper social interaction and training that strengthens other traits that overcome the weaker ones.

All this mumbo-jumbo simply means that not every dog has the ability to be a working dog. A certain breed may be more inclined and have more desirable traits to do a certain job. For example: a Chihuahua has the ability to attack on command and also sniff out narcotics, this does not mean it will make a great working dog for a police officer.

You get a dog from a pound and has the qualities and traits needed for a working dog, it doesn't matter what breed it is, who its parents are, where it came from as long as it has the drive to do the work and suits the needs of the handler, that is the right working dog.

Science and the Brain

It is very important as a handler to have a basic working knowledge of the psychology behind the training of your dog. There is a need for this book to going into great detail on the discoveries of Ian Pavlov and B.F. Skinner.

Although there may be more studies that will help you grasp the science of your craft, these two have laid many valuable principles for you to follow.

There are a lot of misnomers in the K9 industry and if you think about what you're being instructed to do with your dog and it makes sense in human, it will make sense in dog.

Ian Pavlov and his discovery of the function of conditioned reflexes made it possible to study all psychic activity objectively, instead of resorting to subjective methods; it was now possible to investigate by experimental means the most complex interrelations between an organism and its external environment.

Reinforcement or Punishment

With a dog there are two ways in which it's brain stores information. Information concerning the relationship of one event to another. When Pavlov's dogs heard a bell each time they were fed, they soon learned to salivate simply at the sound of the bell. They were "conditioned" to respond to the bell's ring by salivating, and this is called the brain's "conditioned response".

B. F. Skinner invented the operant conditioning chamber, also known as the Skinner box. His studies were more about establishing that free will was actually an illusion and the actions were the result of the consequences of that same action.

Basically what his theory is: if the consequences of an action were bad there is a high chance that the action would not be repeated; and on the flipside if an action received a positive result the action that led to it would be reinforced. He called this the "Principal of reinforcement".

Reinforcement or punishment are used to either increase or decrease the probability that a behavior will occur again in the future. This is how you train a dog; you reinforced behavior you like and correct the behavior you don't like.

Reinforcement is the grease behind the concept a behaviorism and essentially the center and the shaping control of behavior. There are misconceptions that negative reinforcement means punishment.

Social creatures learn best with positive reinforcement, however negative reinforcement strengthens the behavior by removal or avoidance of some aversive event.

Both types of reinforcement strengthen behavior, or increase probability of a behavior reoccurring; the difference is in whether the reinforcing event is rewarding or something that is correcting. This is where genetics can assist or deter the kind of behavior you are looking for in a working dog.

Extinction of a behavior is rarely seen that is compounded by genetics. For example: an alcoholic may be 20 years sober but will always be an alcoholic, the behavior is never extinct. A dog that is timid by nature (genetics) can be trained to overcome the shortcomings, but the behavior will never be extinct.

We essentially train dogs using operant conditioning. This is schedules of reinforcement that are an important part of learning process. When and how often we reinforce the behavior we are looking for has a dramatic impact on the strength and the rate of response.

When it comes dog training there are no trade secrets. Everything we do is based off of the discoveries outlined above. Personal belief cannot change these rules, as some feel that positive reinforcement is the only way to train a dog.

According to what we just read, any time we are not correcting the dog; we are positively reinforcing the dog. Some trainers like to utilize negative reinforcement as their method of training, however, any time you're not correcting the dog you are utilizing positive reinforcement.

Age Comparison

Dogs mature differently to the human, mostly because they age faster than we do. It is important to understand the age of your dog's social concept more so than in years, because your dog just like a human perceives things differently at different stages of their life.

A dog is only a puppy for very brief time of its life and you reward and correct differently based on where the dog is socially. Between its birth in three months the dog is essentially an infant entrained by its mother.

Humans become the teacher around three months of age in the dog which is equal to that of a five-year-old socially. The dog is learning at this stage but shouldn't be pushed to do complicated tasks. If it were a human this is where we teach basic manners and should also be done with your dog. Most humans start seeing problems develop within their dog between the ages of four months and six months, this is the preteen and teenage of your dog social life; and if you think about it as a human were most of our adult problems started.

This is important to understand as you have to reward and correct your dog according to their social abilities not to the amount of years on earth. As a human will reward a 13-year-old much differently than an eight-year-old; the same rule applies to our dog.

Real Age of Dog	Human Years
3 months	5 years
6 months	10 years
1 year	15 years
2 years	24 years
4 years	32 years
6 years	40 years
8 years	48 years
10 years	56 years
14 years	72 years
18 years	88-91 years *
20 years	91-96 years*
21 years	96-106 years*

Your dog has an internal clock that can be very accurate. This is known as body rhythms, but also must be understood when it comes to the schedule of reinforcement.

We know that our dogs are pattern animals, and they learn through positive and negative reinforcement and that schedule of reinforcement is very important to the dog's ability to learn the task in which we are trying to teach them.

Timing is everything when teaching a dog. The time that we as humans have isn't as accelerated as the time of which a dog perceives things. Seconds to humans can be minutes to a dog, we can't correct for something that happened five minutes ago and think that our dog will put the two together. If you don't catch the dog on the moment a reward is in the reward and a correction won't be a correction.

Body rhythms can affect your dog's mindset in training, as your dog internally knows it's time to eat and their brain is focused on eating not learning. The same goes for having to go to the bathroom, you as a handler should know when your dog has to go. It is hard to learn when you have to go to the bathroom.

Realizing that things like knowing that it is dinner time, or time for the bathroom will affect the working abilities of your partner. Do we as humans work well when we are hungry or need to utilize the facilities? Just because your partner had a chance to take a break, before you went to training, or conducted its daily rituals, doesn't mean that they don't have to go again.

You can eliminate this problem by giving your partner a break before entering a working environment, even if the dog stops to mark territory, it is done outside. Don't mistake your dog marking territory as the same thing.

Feed your dog in the morning and again in the evening on a set schedule, and you can aid in eliminating most of the scrounging problems. You should also take food to work in the event your shift takes you past feeding time, as your dog will be more interested in eating than working.

SIX

The Senses

We talked about how a dog communicates. Communication is an in and out process that is detected through their senses. Senses are physiological capacities of organism which provide data for interpretation. Humans have a multitude of senses even many similar to animals, but we utilize them differently.

A big part of understanding your dog is understanding its senses and accepting that they are indeed different than humans. Both humans and dogs have the same five senses: sight, hearing, taste, touch and smell, however while most humans primarily utilize their sense of hearing and seeing; dogs primarily utilize their sense of smelling and visual but also utilize their touch and hearing better than you can imagine.

Smell

Scent is undoubtedly the most important of the dog's practical senses but also the most difficult for us to comprehend. Odors have a powerful influence on both the physiology and the behavior of the dog. Smell memories last for life and affect almost all canine behaviors, and you should always remember this and remember the impact it will have on your training.

The dog's ability to smell the world around him and to interpret these smells depends upon a complicated chemical sensing system. Puppies have heat sensors in their noses to help find their mother during the time when their eyes and ears are closed. These sensors disappear by the time they are adults.

Their mobile nostrils help them determine the direction of the scent. Sniffing is different from breathing as one of every three breaths is for sent. The septal organ most sensitive part of the dog's nose and responsible for initiating sniffing behavior.

When a dog is overheated and actively panting, its sense of smell is reduced by as much as 40 percent as it uses the air to cool itself rather than for smelling.

While a dog's brain is only one-tenth the size of a human brain, the part that controls smell is 40 times larger than in humans. A dog's sense of smell is about 1,000 to 10,000,000 times more sensitive than a human's (depending on the breed). A human has about 5 million scent glands, compared to a dog, who has anywhere from 125 million to 300 million (depending on the breed).

The average dog has such acutely sensitive scenting ability that it can detect and identify smells that are so dilute that even the most sensitive of scientific instruments cannot measure them.

There is no difference between a dogs looking for explosives, narcotics, bedbugs, humans, animals, or anything else that hasn't odor for which we wanted to find; they are hunting.

Sight

Puppies are born blind and generally gain their vision within the first two weeks. Dogs are not exactly color blind, meaning they do not only see in shades of only black and white. Studies have shown that dogs see in colors of various shades of blue and yellow.

Dogs can see best at dusk and dawn. Their low-light vision is much better than a human's, but their overall vision is not better. Dogs cannot see as well at a distance as the average human and humans can also see things close up better; dogs can recognize objects better when they are moving and sometimes overlook the same object when it is still. Dogs see images on a TV screen, but most likely also see a rapidly flickering light, almost like a strobe light.

Hearing

When we talk about hearing in our dogs is important to understand the dogs physical capabilities, but would like to remind you that in Pavlov utilized the dogs hearing or tone to prove his theories.

This means your dog's hearing is very important to training your dog and more importantly your tone, tone, tone, tone. A dog's hearing is estimated to be four times more acute than ours. A misleading statement for in fact dogs can actually hear sounds from four times the distance we can but still hear the sounds in a broadly similar fashion.

However, dogs are better at detecting higher notes than we are. The range of hearing for a few species is like this: Man up to 20,000 cps Dog up to 40,000 cps Cat up to 45,000 cps Bat 30-98,000 cps Dolphin 100-130,000 cps. The acuteness of a dog's hearing ranges over about eight and a half octaves, the same as us (compared to ten octaves over which a cat can hear).

Pavlov was the first scientist to investigate pitch discrimination in dogs and showed that a dog can distinguish two notes differing by only one eighth of a tone. This is the science behind which we will establish tone variations for no, good, okay, and done. This science established that a dog can distinguish between tone variations and if we paired them with a physical action a dog can distinguish that one "NO" is different from another "NO".

Dogs have 18 or more muscles in their ears allowing them to be mobile, whereas a human has only 6 and can only move their ears slightly, if at all. Dogs with perked ears can usually hear better than dogs with hanging ears, especially if they can move their ears in the direction of the sound.

Touch

Touch remains forever the most potent reward that a dog can receive, more important than even food.

Stroking a mature dog that knows you can reduce its heart rate, lower blood pressure and drop skin temperature. In other words, stroking reduces the dog's state of arousal. (The same thing happens to us too. Stroke a dog to which you have formed an attachment and your state of arousal also diminishes.) The opposite is also true of an exciting stroke can also cause your dog to be more excited.

In common with many other mammals but not us, dogs have special sensory hairs, vibrissae, above their eyes below their jaws and, most importantly, on their muzzles. These sensory hairs are imbedded in areas of skin that have intense blood supplies and numerous nerve endings. Dogs can sense air flow and current with their vibrissae as well as determine the shape and texture of objects. Of course, the dog's entire body has sensory never endings that are stimulated by touch. These can sometimes respond in an abnormal way and cause common behavioral disorder.

Under this principle, a dog can sense our slightest movements, air pressure changes that can include training aids that are cold in a warm environment, thus something as simple as a change of temperature can alert the canine to something different, then lead them to respond to the desired odor. From a philosophical view, did the dog alert to the change in temperature or the odor itself?

Taste

We humans have around 9,000 taste buds on our tongues whereas a dog is estimated to have 1706. Most of these are on the anterior portion of the tongue.

It has always been assumed that dogs share the human taste world and, although they have taste buds like us that register sweet, sour, bitter, salty, they do so in such a unique way that it is probably better to discuss a dog's taste sensation as "pleasant – indifferent – unpleasant". Taste doesn't really affect your dog's working ability.

Six Sense

The question still remains as to whether dogs have a sixth sense. What we can put together from all of the different senses of the dog, are that they are the same senses as a human, but the dog has survived evolution by utilizing all of their senses all of the time.

They can and do pick up on the little differences you as a handler will make, such as changing your tone, heart beating faster, nervous behaviors, and when paired with an action can become a learned behavior.

Hormones

Take for example the situation of the dominant male dog, the leader of the pack. (With pet dogs, the pack, regrettably, is often the human household in which he lives.) Outwardly it would appear that the dog has become dominant because he has a high level of the male sex hormone, testosterone.

But all is not as it outwardly seems. A dog is not born with the genetic blueprint to have a high testosterone level. Rather, it is the circumstances of his existence, which teat he claims as his own, how his siblings and his mother treat him when he is young, how his human guardians treat and train him when he is older, all of these behavioral factors that affect the level of stress under which he lives.

The dog that copes best with stress is the dog that becomes a natural leader, and the natural leader is then entitled to increase his testosterone level to help him maintain his position of authority. Technically, the phenomenon is called biofeedback.

Your dog treats and communicates with you as a pack member. As the handler you have the ability to condition him to become what he is or will be. Dogs will look to you for leadership, either you lead or they will, and if you lead, you must lead in the way of the dog not the human. The basic genetic code of dog utilizes structure, discipline, compassion, guidance, and order.

Realize that there is a difference between behavior and shaping behavior. Behavior is the dog's natural social traits, and shaping behavior is bringing out traits.

Dogs need testosterone in order to develop normal male behavior patterns but they also need to learn how to behave as males. An intact male dog that has never mated with a female can find it difficult, if not impossible, to differentiate between a female dog's head or vulva or his owner's arm.

Male dogs that have been castrated and have no circulating testosterone, however, will continue to successfully mount and mate even though testosterone has virtually completely disappeared from the bloodstream within a day of castration. There is a belief in the K9 Industry that castration takes the drive from the dog. The decision to castrate your dog should be made from an educated view rather than one handed down from belief. Castration before a certain age has been proven to decrease the likelihood of related issues.

The drive of a dog is effected by castration. An intact male will be forced to deal with conflicting odors because his testosterone is dictating to the dog when it must do. In many years that I and my wife have worked dogs for detection, personal protection, tracking, agility, obedience and the military and US customs; we have seen a vast number of working dogs that were intact and later neutered. Not one time did the neutering diminish the drive of the dog, if anything it increased the dogs ability to focus as it didn't have to deal with this surges of testosterone.

There is also a myth in the K9 industry concerning sexual activity with emotional behavior. Your dog having had a sexual experience does not make it emotionally more stable. This is in the mind of the human not the dog. To say that sexual experience through dog will make it more emotionally stable is no different than saying a human having sexual experience will make it emotionally more stable.

Castration only takes away the dogs ability to produce testosterone. It will not make them less frustrated, change their overall demeanor or its ability to work. Either your dog has drive to start with or it doesn't; while testosterone will in fact increase your dog's overall drive in a fight, it is not generally the kind you are looking for.

The Behavior Effects of Estrogen And Testosterone

Spaying and neutering a dog does affect their working abilities. It can reduce roaming up to 90%; inter-male mail aggression up to 60%; mounting people up to 60% and some decline in mounting bitches in heat too, urine marking in the house can also be reduced up to 50%.

Castration does not change a dog's personality, nor does it interfere with the abilities of working dogs whether they are service, hunting or guard dogs.

Castration doesn't influence the dog's relationship with people either, except that it is ultimately more likely that the castrated dog will accept authority more readily from his human pack members than he would have before castration. It is also been established that the age of castration is not terribly important. The same effects will be seen at virtually all stages of the dog's life regardless of exactly when he is castrated.

Spaying female dogs, on the other hand, is a common procedure, carried out to prevent unwanted litters but equally to control the behavioral effects of the twice yearly surges in the female hormones estrogen and progesterone.

A male dog lives with a constant supply of male hormone circulating in his body and influencing his mind. Females on the other hand only become under sex hormone influence twice yearly for a total of four months.

Behavioral changes as mentioned above are why working dogs are spayed or neutered. It is important to realize that such minor things can and do affect you're partners working mindset and abilities. A bitch in heat can override any canine's ability to listen to you, however, this doesn't mean they can't and won't work; just that it is a factor you need to work through.

Puberty does not signify emotional maturity. Some dogs can be mature long before puberty. Others will not mature until sometime after. Your dog will not automatically change because they had a year mark. Reward and correct your dog based on their social age and overall demeanor, not their human age.

Patrick Currey

SEVEN

The Pack Mentality

We have seen the evidence that the domestic dog and the wolf are closer genetically than the wolf and coyote and one must understand that if this relation is so close, they have a lot in common. With this in mind, let us look at how our wild brothers communicate, but first we must try to look at life through our partner's eyes.

You can learn a lot from watching your dog interact with other dogs, or watching wolf behavior. Learning that a dog will always be a dog, no matter what its job is, will help you understand more about why they do what they do; think dog first.

The Pack

Gray wolves are extremely social and highly intelligent animals. They typically live in packs, or groups, of 5-10 related animals (most packs actually contain 4-7 animals) which function as a highly cohesive unit. This "pack" is essentially an extended family unit with a very tight social bond. John Theberge, a noted Canadian wolf biologist, has been quoted as saying "Their social bonding and care-giving behavior are second only to those of humans and other social primates".

Our partners are descendants of the wolf and live in packs or groups of 5-10. This "pack" is essentially an extended family unit with a very tight social bond. Let's now try to look at life through our partner's perspective. This implies that we are now part of a pack or extended family to our partner, and a good explanation for why we work so well together as a team.

Hierarchy

Regardless of whether you want to believe it or not, there is and always will be a hierarchy in your dog's mind.

This is a trait of evolution and your dog much like a human are born with everything they have as far as social traits.

Domestic dogs are very similar to their cousins the wolf when it comes to hierarchy. At the top there is the alpha and at the bottom there is the omega. In the wild these positions are very important and have a dramatic impact on the social behaviors of the pack; this structure is not voted on and is constantly up for challenge.

The amount of dogs in the home do not mean there will or will not be a hierarchy issue. Humans may not see or pay attention to the subtle hierarchy challenges and others may experience the full brunt of these challenges. Because you have a working dog does not mean they are the alpha dog. Always remember is not the size and the dog fight but the size of the fight in the dog.

Hierarchy in our domestic domain is very important to pay attention to as it exists in your dog's life and will affect its working abilities.

Taking a lower ranking dog out of the household, or paying more attention to it will cause ripples within the hierarchy structure. This can lead to problems in the working venues if you are not paying attention to the subtle behaviors of the other dogs within your home as you leave and return.

Various body positions and movements, intimidation and harassment enforce the social rank of our dogs. They have very expressive faces and often communicate through subtle gestures of the mouth, ears and eyes even position of the tail is also used to communicate posture.

Who gets fed first, attention, sleeping arrangements, marking in the yard, toys, who goes in and out of the doors first and pretty much anything your dog determines will influence the hierarchy.

From observing my own structures over the years, I have seen many differences within a domestic pack structure than what studies have shown from wild pack structures. In the wild the alpha is always top in every situation, but in domestic format one dog can be alpha outside and omega inside the home. We as humans directly influenced this, as we are and should always be the pack leader; sadly in most cases the dog is running the pack.

It is not as important to determine which of your dogs is the alpha, although it is not hard to figure out. Various body positions and movements, intimidation and harassment to enforce the social rank of your pack. Communication through facial expressions and subtle gestures of the mouth ears, eyes and even the position of the tail communicates.

Patrick Currey

EIGHT

Science Of Training And Learning

Let's just take a moment to break this down into laymen terms that we can associate with what we are trying to accomplish. We will associate with detection work, as this should be the easiest to understand. It really applies to any type of detection work, there is no difference between a dog looking for explosives, narcotics, bed bugs, humans, animals, or anything else that has an odor for which we want them to find; they are hunting.

• **Conditional Reflex** (Teaching) - regarded as a fundamental aspect of learning and suggests that this is how our partner learns. This would be where we teach the dog to pair the desired response with the act of searching for an odor.

• **Conditional Stimulus** (Odor) - The odor we are introducing for our partner to detect for us, be it narcotics, explosives or human sent.

• **Unconditional Stimulus** (Reward) - Valued reward our partner receives upon finding the desired odor. Keep in mind, that this is our partner's paycheck.

• **Unconditional Response** (Alert) - or change in behavior the dog gives when it detects odor. You may see this when your dog is taking a break sniffing for the great place to go, then franticly searches for a specific area that has just passed the nose. Remember, an "Alert" is a noticeable change of behavior in your dog.

• **Conditional Response** (Response) - response we have assigned our partner for showing us the location of the desired odor. "Bite-n-Scratch" (Positive Response), "Sit" (Passive Response).

• **Positive Reinforcers** (Any type of reward) - praises to motivate our partner to keep the hunt going. "Good dog, find it" or extreme praise for the finding the odor, with desired response on its own.

- **Negative Reinforcers** (Anything the dogs sees as bad) - when introducing odor in the beginning stages of training, it is vitally important to avoid at all cost any negatives. This can become extremely difficult, as we send so many messages to our partner and we can't always tell what they construe as a negative.

You may ask why it is so important for us to understand communication as our partner sees it, and I can only tell you that all the years I have been working with dogs, most handlers and trainers have no care or clue why. Others will follow blindly and work and teach as they have been taught, again believing that they are leading the right path, and this is why you must have a least a minimal understanding of your partners mind and how it affects your work.

Unconditional and Conditional Response

In a typical experiment, Pavlov showed that if the presentation of food to a dog was repeatedly accompanied by the sound of a bell, then the dog would come to respond to the bell as if it were food. Pavlov measured the salivary response to paired presentations of food and bell and then measured salivation in response to presentation of the bell alone. He regarded salivation to the food as an "**Unconditional Response**." And the subsequent salivation to the bell alone as a "**Conditional Response**". Because it is 'conditional' upon prior pairing between food and bell. He suggested that the cells of the 'Central-Nervous-System' changed structurally and chemically during conditioning, (And this notion is not too far removed from the modern view).

When he signaled the delivery of food by ringing a bell, the behavior of the dog towards the stimulus, (The bell), gradually changed. The animal began by orientating to the bell, licking its lips and salivating. When Pavlov recorded the salivation by placing a small tube in the salivary duct and collecting the saliva, he found that the amount of the saliva collected increased as the animal experienced more pairings between the sound of the bell, and food presentation. It appeared that the dog had learned to associate the bell with the food.

Pavlov referred to the bell as the "**Conditional Stimulus.**" And to the food as the "**Unconditional Stimulus.**" Salivation in response to presentation of food was called the "**Unconditional Response**", while salivation in response to the bell was called the "**Conditional Response.**"

After a number of pairings, the bell alone is enough to cause salivation. The bell is then known as the "**Conditional Stimuli**" because as a result of its 'training,' the dog salivates if and when the stimulus is presented. Similarly, the salivation response to the bell is known as the "**Conditional Response.**" Conditioning experiments that apply motivationally beneficial, or **Positive Reinforcers** like the unconditional stimulus (the food), are examples of **Positive Conditioning**.

Conditional reflexes can also be established in experiments that employ Negative Reinforcers, such as electric shock, which the animal tries to avoid.

Punishment and Praise

"A reinforcer is characterized not so much by its intrinsic properties as a stimulus but by its motivational significance to the animal" (i.e. Enjoys praise, dislikes punishment) (Positive and Negative Reinforcers will be discussed shortly).

Clever Hans – A Scientific Warning This section is paramount to establish to handlers that "**the dog does and will look for cues from the handler**". Every working dog does this and handlers need to know it, but it needs to be shortened and easier to understand.

In the late 1800 and early 1900's Ian Pavlov published his findings on the function of conditioned reflexes. During the early 20th century, there was a huge interest in animal intelligence due largely to the publications of Charles Darwin.

During this same timeframe a man named Wilhelm von Osten; a German mathematics teacher, a horse trainer and what some thought of as a mystic owned a horse called "Hans".

The taught talents of his horse brought worldwide attention. Hans was said to have been taught to add, subtract, multiply, work fractions, tell time, keep track of the calendar, musical tones even to read and spell with an understanding of the German language.

Von Osten would ask Hans questions to which he would answer by tapping his hoof in reply; it didn't even matter whether the questions were written or spoken.

Von Osten toured throughout Germany showing off Hans' talent. In 1904 the New York Times reported these abilities and the new phenomenon created investigation as a result of the ensuing public interest. The German board of education appointed philosopher and psychologist Carl Stumpf and 13 others to include a veterinarian, circus manager, a Calvary officer, a number of school teachers and the director of the Berlin to a logical gardens.

Pfungst tested the basis for these claimed abilities by isolating the horse and questioners from spectators to ensure no cues could come from them. They also used others to question that were not those of Von Osten. They utilized varying questions known and unknown to the questioners and also utilize blinders to vary whether the horse could see the question.

During these trials they discovered that the horse could get the correct answer even if Von Osten didn't ask the question. This ruled out the possibility of fraud, however, the horse could only get the right answer if the questioner knew the answer before the question was asked and could also see the questioner.

They also observed that when von Osten knew the answers to the questions the horse was 89% and only 6% when he did not. This led them to then examine the behavior of the questionnaire in detail. They then discovered while the horses tapping approach the right answer Von Osten's posture and even his facial expressions changed in ways consistent to the release of tension as the horse made the final and correct tap.

The subtle changes subsequently provided a cue to the horse telling to stop tapping. Much like that of our working dogs, a horse has a social communication system that depends on the detection of small postural changes and explain why the horse could easily pick up on the cues given even if they were done subconsciously.

The investigation concluded in 1907, and demonstrated that the horse was not actually performing the mental tasks, rather it was watching the reaction of its human observer. Pfungst conclusively demonstrated that if he stood in front of the horse and without asking anything, he could make it tap its hoof and stand to attention by slightly nodding and straightening his head. What may have appeared to be actions of great intelligence approved to be a horse simply reading and interpreting what it thought the handler wanted it to do to solve the problem, even though the trainer was unaware he was providing such cues.

This became known as the clever Hans effect and has become very important in the later studies of animal cognition. Even after the official debunking of Hans' abilities Von Osten continued to show Hans' abilities throughout Germany.

This discovery affected how animals are now tested in isolated apparatus without human interaction. This in itself created a problem of its own, because the most interesting phenomena in animal cognition are most likely to be demonstrated in that of a social context which means it is important to create a social relationship between the trainer and animal.

This finding is very important to the K9 industry. As a trainer or a handler one must determine if the dog knows the material or simply studying the test. All too often humans inadvertently cue behaviors in their working dog.

A study by the University of California Davis established that subtle cues can be telegraphed by the handler to the dog resulting in a default positive.

Patrick Currey

NINE

Leadership

Over the years it has become more of a cliché to talk about leadership and it's important to the working dog world. Being a good leader is essential part that will transform an average working dog team to a great one. Leadership comes in many different ways, from many different things in your life, it is also continue to evolve and expand as you grow as a team.

What does a good leader have to do with being a good working dog team? You as handler are ultimately responsible for how well your dog does and does not do in both training and a working environment.

A good handler evolves from a good trainer, any good trainer should also be a good leader to you as a team.

Quality training over quantity is a good mindset that have. Many trainers in this industry are self-appointed; titles, positions, years as a handler, training attended, number of dogs work or any other statistic don't mean anything if you are not producing results.

A good trainer should be able to articulate what they are teaching you, it's importance and relevance to future training and working. They should also be teaching you how to become the leader of your dog, as you are the one holding the leash.

Understanding how a dog thinks and why a dog does something is important, but the one holding the leash is the one that's leading the show. A handler has to be able to communicate to their canine what to do, how do, as long as needed, in any environment until they say stop.

The working dog is a product of the one holding the leash. All excuses aside, your dog is behaving the way you showed it to.

What you are saying or what you are being told is either an excuse or a reason, if you sit back and listen from an objective point of view to find more excuses than reasons in the K9 industry.

Looking back on the leaders that I had to learn from, were not the greatest examples to follow, but even a poorly leader still has something to be learned from. Ultimately you learn more from watching poor leadership skills then you will from positive leadership skills, because most the time a good leader doesn't have to make an effort to be one.

The greatest part of being a working dog handler, is the same as the worst part of being a working dog handler; you alone are the one responsible. Just because you don't know what you're doing doesn't validate your excuse, find someone that can teach you how to do things right. This book has already outlined the only two rules you have to follow, it is now up to you of how to present that material to your dog.

In order to become a good leader, one must continually keep the lines of communication open. When it comes to being a K9 Handler you will hear many opinions of the working dog industry. A good piece of advice would be to take every opinion and store it in the good or bad section of your mind, apply the good and don't utilize the bad. In order for you to advance in this art form you should expect to fail before you become great, while remembering that patience is a virtue that is most needed to become great.

It is never bad to make mistakes, unless you keep making the same one over and over, and that is why leadership is so important to your partner working for you. It is very important to start thinking and leading like a dog, as that is the only way they understand. Dogs don't lead with words; they lead with actions, posture, and force.

Dogs don't just accept leadership, it is earned.
To earn leadership in your dog's mind, you must truly lead in a manner they understand.

Right now, I want you to think back to every boss you have ever worked for. How many of them would you want to work for again? How many would you like to toss out a window? How many have you worked for that you would follow to the ends of the earth? Not many of us can say that we have ever worked for the latter boss, but we have all had one or two that we will never forget.

Most of you have never been in a leadership role and it is your job to learn how you can become a competent and effective leader to your partner. First you must believe in your abilities as a leader and the task you're trying to accomplish. You can't grow as a leader if you're not willing to take a risk and try something new just because you might fail.

Lead by example

Look and act the part, as your partner is a "show me" kind of follower. If you are confident or at least look the part, you are halfway there to being a good leader.

A good leader rewards accordingly. You shouldn't reward your partner the same every time, as not every accomplishment is equal. A reward must always be given in some form, but not all rewards have to be physical. Is a smile or thumbs-up not a reward to us? Then a good boy, quick rub are a reward to the dog, and rewards aren't just when they find something, because time is different to a dog than a human, so a good dog while working is necessary to keep the motivation level up.

Be Honest in your Training

You can lie to a lot of people, but I can promise you that you can't lie to your dog. This means that you can't fake your way through the different levels of training, because your partner will know what you're doing and follow your lead. Take all criticism as constructive and always ask yourself "what am I doing to cause this"?

Our dogs expect leaders to have a sense of direction and an understanding of what you are teaching them. During the basic stages of training a dog, a little light bulb turns on. For each dog and handler this comes at a different time, but none the less it happens in order to progress during the training.

The bulb starts getting brighter and brighter as the canine progresses, and then all of a sudden the dog understands your communication begins to effectively learn.

Understand and utilize the fact your dog has survived by utilizing all of its senses at one time versus individually or a few at a time like we do. Knowing how powerful the dogs sense of touch is, means they can tell the difference between you having an open handed leash or a firm grip.

With the exception of reward or correcting behavior, training a dog is not governed by a set of rules; there are no absolutes. You have to think outside of the box, to coin a phrase, and continually expound on the new skills the dog has learned once they have become proficient.

In order for the dog to work for you, they must believe that you are competent to guide them where you as a team are headed. They must see the leader as capable and effective. If they doubt the leader's abilities, they are unlikely to effectively follow you.

Trust is not given, it is earned. To earn your partner's trust you have to show them you know what you're talking about by actions not words. You need to work each day like you are the CEO of a company of one. Your dog is the employee and you are the boss. To be an effective boss, you must have an understanding of the job, proficiently teach what is expected then establish a work ethic.

Mark my words, you will never find another job working for someone else that gives you the opportunity to have total control over something like dog training does. Coaching from your trainer only goes so far; your desire to become successful relies upon your shoulders alone.

A leader must be able to communicate in a manner the dog understands. You have to learn to properly read your dog's language, then apply the appropriate reward or correction for the behavior you are dealing with. Even our dogs long to find some greater sense of purpose and worth in their day-to-day working lives. Although the enthusiasm, energy, and positive attitude of a good leader may not change the content of work, they certainly can make the context more meaningful, so you must always find ways to build confidence in the dog's knowledge of the job.

Patrick Currey

TEN

Rewarding

In the infancy of training, rewarding your dog starts out to be a simple process. The dog responds, reward is given end of story, yet it must evolve into much, much more.

Think of it in the form of money. We as humans work for money, but if we do not value money they cannot be rewarding. Bill Gates said he would lose money if he were to stop to pick-up a hundred dollar bill lying on the ground. This is not to say that money doesn't matter to him, just that he has grown to value money in a different way now.

We as humans work for a paycheck, or we wouldn't work, your dog is no different except they don't value money. The reward that you give your dog essentially doesn't matter as long as it's rewarding to them.

There's a lot of controversy in the K9 industry over what is the best reward for a dog. Food, ball, tug are all viable rewards for a dog, but no matter what you use if you do not continue to make it rewarding to them the desire for the dog to work will diminish.

Rewarding is probably the most important aspect of training any dog but especially a working dog. Your dog already knows how to do all of the tasks you wanted to learn, the trick is you have to show them that they're doing those tasks for something that is rewarding to them.

The first step is to find what your dog values the most and show them that you give the reward for the desired task. Giving a dog ate food reward that doesn't value food as much as a ball or a tug makes no sense. You can also make a case for starving a dog so that it work for food; is a dog working to overcome hunger or because it enjoys what it's doing.

Most of the rewards that you will be doing with your dog do not have to be monetary in nature; simple "good dog" or physical stroke can keep it dog content until they find what you've asked them to find. You must also understand that not all actions deserve the same rewards no matter what it is your dog is doing. Essentially you must teach your dog work ethic; i.e. you get paid for how you work.

The first day of your new job become an early work a little late to give 100% the entire day. Your employer pulls out $1000 cash and hands it to you for a job well done. The following day you wake up late and arrive 10 minutes after the workday starts. Your drained from the day before and work about 75% the entire day, as well as asking your employer to go home early. In turn, they pull out a thousand dollars cash and hand it to you for a job well done. The question here is what time you get a come to work how much of an effort to put in the next day? Most social creatures would learn that they don't have to work half as hard to get the same pay. Your dog is no different, we learned from Hans that they can learn to cheat and from Skinner that they have work ethic.

It is your job as a handler to instill that work ethic and to ensure they are being paid properly for the work done.

No matter what you use for a reward your dog will always value that it's coming from you. Most often handlers utilizing ball and food reward fail to interact along with the reward, where is a tug reward pass at handler interaction. Always remember "It's not a Reward, unless it is a Reward". Play the game the dog wants to play not the one you feel is rewarding.

In our human workforce, the only thing that your boss needs to give you is your paycheck for you coming to work, nothing more, nothing less. It wouldn't take long before you started not enjoying the place, looking for other work or just go with the flow of the mindless drivel. We thrive as social creatures on social interactions with their coworkers; your dog is no different.

Many handlers improperly reward their dog; most feel that the only time they need to reward is when they find something. Our dogs sense of time is different from ours, a social reward along the way at the appropriate time is vital. Humans need inspiration to fulfill themselves in their job and so does a dog. Something as simple as having a sense of accomplishment or feeling appreciated we can all relate to, so feel like you can't praise your dog for not finding something as well. This doesn't name reward your dog with a ball, tug, or food, just some simple praise and maybe a physical touch will do wonders.

Don't be Afraid to Express Yourself

Your dog will see that you're faking it, if you don't lead from the heart. This will bring problems in the future as the canine's natural lead or follow instinct will take over. That or they will just shut down and go through the motions of the job, much like someone you know. When working with a handler one day, the dog was struggling to understand how the task was to be done. All of a sudden the dog finally got it and perform the task perfectly, however, the handlers reward was very basic and plain.

There was no excitement, no over joy for the dog and what they had accomplished, just a plain good girl and a small kibble of food.

I discussed in great lengths with the handler about being over joyous at times like this and the impact it will have on the dog and its work ethic. When I asked the handler why didn't they take the opportunity to reward accordingly, the handler looked at me and simply said "oh, was she just knows" and walked away. The dog doesn't just know, you have to teach it.

Working a dog is an art, and takes time to hone your abilities as a handler and for your dog to become a stronger worker. You need to learn to find the right tone, touch and even body language for the each situation.

One of the handlers I was working with struggled meeting the certification standards. They became very frustrated after several failed attempts and wanted to continue training. The problem was the dog knew all the required odors, so that wasn't an issue and also knew what to do when it found odor; so what was the problem. The question that should be asked, what is the problem then?

During our time together I continually emphasized the importance of the reward to the dog. The handler continued to poorly reward the dog and the dog ultimately became frustrated and didn't like working for the handler. Instead of doing more detection training, I had to physically show the handler how to properly reward the dog. The next attempt at certification resulted in a positive and the handler never failed another certification.

It cannot be emphasized enough how important the reward is to a working dog and more importantly reward accordingly. You can't reward the same for poor work as you do excellent work; the performance of the dog should determine the value of the reward presented.

Observing Others

You have to observe other teams working; you can learn more from a poor handler than from watching an experienced one. Watching another teams work will also show you fault within yourself, as you can see that what you thought was nothing, actually was an alert from your dog.

It can also confirm that you are on the right track, but either way you log a memory that will be useful to help you not make the same mistake twice. Don't ever stop taking in an outsider's view, by reading, training or seminars. I have argued many of times that I was not doing an action to which I was being accused, only to watch myself do exactly that on video.

See Yourself

Your partner will be the first to hear this, and you may never notice the true effect it has.

Your tone of voice is one of the most important tools you have. To make your tone effective you must teach the dog what each tone means. This is the one venue handlers understand from the first day, yet still struggle years after they have been taught the principles behind it. Utilize your tone to your benefit, it is your greatest strength and weakness, depending on you and what you put into it.

Exactly like clicker training you can use your different tones of voice or noises to correct or reward the dog during a behavior. All too often I find handlers utilizing the same tone for good as they use for something bad and the tone actually cancels itself out to mean nothing.

In order for the dog not to pattern our actions we need to continually send them the message that the only constant there is, is the odor they are trained to find and nothing else, thus the pattern will be that there are no patterns.

The only exception to this is in the beginning stages of operant conditioning as we want the dog to learn the behavior we are trying to teach, then worry about our tells later.

Having a clear understanding is a necessary first step, yet the ability to consistently deliver the message and act on it requires a high level of skill.

Before you can do the right things, you have to know how to do them, with your dog this means you have to have a goal for your training and work on that goal; perfect then vary; then perfect the variations, then move to a higher level.

Your job as the leader is to teach the message and ensure it is completely understood, and then give the dog the opportunity to prove they understand the message by allowing them to make mistakes and showing them you are there to help them when they need it. Mistakes must happen to learn and are only bad if you don't learn from them, so create the opportunity to let your dog work as the leader to show confidence in them.

See What the Dog Sees

There are many available tools you can use to take a look at yourself. For example, the video camera will become a big eye opener.

We will utilize this during training, not for the purpose of keeping records of the training, but as a tool for you to see what others see you doing. And most importantly, what your partner is seeing you do. You must ask yourself after each day; "How did my partner see me as a boss today?"

"Being a good leader is not something that casually occurs. It takes great thought, care, insight, commitment, and energy. When it all comes together, it brings out the best of who you are." -Mary Godwin, Radius

---

This above statement needs to be ingrained in your head. It is the basis for which you will lead and train your partner, as this is an **Art Form** not just dog training. You will have days that you are severely frustrated at yourself and your partner, and it may seem that it will never come together. With patience, time, and proper training you will reap what you sow.

Compelling words may be essential to lifting your dog's spirits, but leaders know that their dogs are more deeply moved by deeds. Dogs expect leaders to act, to pay attention to every aspect through their mind. Leaders take every opportunity to prove their position to the pack. Leading by example is how a wild dog runs the pack. If the alpha allows a pack member to be attacked wrongfully, it fails as a leader and if you allow your dog to act in a negative behavior you are not a leader in their eyes.

When it comes to rewarding the dog, the reward alone is not what your partner works for. They ultimately are working to please you; the reward is the icing on the cake. In the same token, you can negatively get your dog to make the wrong decision to please you. This is **"negative pleasing"** is learned through patterns; it is your deeds or **"PRAISE"**. So make it a fun game and most importantly, one they like.

Sharing Canines Values

This would be the reward. You must ensure that it is always of value to your partner. This is done by the game, in which you must make them believe that they are king when they have the reward.

My last partner Sonny taught me to play the game that he liked. This doesn't mean to keep switching the reward of the dog. If your dog stops finding value in the reward they once had value for, you got bigger problems. All too often, handlers look to find a new reward because the drive of the dog has to work has diminished and as I just stated, you have bigger problems.

Sonny loved to play tug and per direction from my employer that was what I was to do when he found narcotics. That was fine for a while, but he decided that sometimes he liked to play keep the tug away from me, other times he wanted to prance around with it showing it off to others like a prized kill, some days I would just helicopter it straight up for him to catch and repeat. The point is, it was the same reward, just presented differently and most importantly the one the dog wanted.

Align Actions With Values

If you are excited and reward your dog equally across the board for good work habits and the same for bad work habits, the dog will learn it can choose and will ultimately choose to work at the lowest level possible. Work ethic is very important to instill into any workforce, especially a working dog. B.F. Skinner established, through his studies on rats, that a work ethic can be established. It is up to you to set the pace as to how you want your dog to work.

Once people are clear about the leader's values, about their own values, and about shared values, they know what's expected of them. They can manage higher levels of stress, and can better handle the conflicting demands of work and their personal lives. (Leadership Challenge Kouzes/Posner).

To a working dog this is one of the most important skills to be taught. Without words, they use observation to understand an event.

You can't tell a dog that it will be okay, you have to lead them through tough times and show them it will be okay.

A professional athlete trains for as many situations as they can possibly find, and those that are able to generalize one situation into another, are the great ones. You can't always work and train in the same environment, but you can teach your dog how to deal with stress.

I find most behavioral problems stem from owner's dog having extreme stress or no stress at all. You have to show your dog stress is manageable and you must show them you are not going to let them worry about anything, because that is your job.

Think of how comfortable you become with your job, then how you would feel if you were transferred to another office, would you have the same comfort level?

Chances are you wouldn't, just like your partner when they are so many established patterns during training, and the work environment becomes the office transfer.

Expand Your Communication Skills

Reasonable people know that great achievement requires hard work. Let your dog know that you have the utmost confidence in their ability to succeed by using good leash techniques. Micromanaging your dog by not letting them work for what they were employed for just doesn't make sense. The military taught us to block and essentially micromanage our dogs during a search and unfortunately this method has been passed along to many a trainer and handler. This method has many flaws and essentially teaches the dog poor habits, but is an easy way for a handler to quickly learn to work a dog somewhat effective.

Trusting your dog is hard in the beginning and is a two way street. You have to trust that your dog is telling you when nothing is there and also when something is. Just remember, it isn't your dog's job to find the item (odor you taught them to find), it is their job to put you in the right place to look.

Odor is like water and travels in the path of least resistance. I have seen multiple times with multiple dogs on multiple scent venues alert and respond to an area that didn't have the source, but couldn't care less about the true area of source.

Just because you can't find something doesn't mean your canine is wrong.

For example: Sonny walked over 4lbs of marijuana in a waterless toilet during training at a defunct hotel. However, he was searching the outside area like there were narcotics outside. After all the dogs walked the same training aid, I started to use my brain and deducted that the odor was being pulled like a vacuum outside through the air vent, which is why he was searching so frantically with no success outside.

This doesn't open the door for the handler excuses. While there might be residual odor available to the dog, it is not an excuse as to why the dog is alerting. The handler excuse book needs to be tossed out and handlers need to listen to what they are telling others, because when someone feels they are hearing an excuse, it is likely an excuse.

Sonny didn't alert to a package that the postal inspectors felt very confident had narcotics; they just needed a K9 to get a search warrant to open the package. We ran and re-ran the package with not the slightest alert or change of behavior on any package in the line, let alone the one they were suspect of.

I mentioned to the senior agent that just because the dog didn't alert to the package, doesn't mean that there weren't narcotics in it; No odor available equals no alert.

We separated the package in a narcotics free vault and I ran another line with the suspect package the following day; beautiful alert/response. There was 10lbs of marijuana encased in a metal pot, sealed with silicone caulk, washed and then placed in a box that was spray foamed.

This was estimated to have been done only a short time before it was put into the mail system and arrived to our location.

> *Odor simply didn't have enough time to permeate through all of the layers, but when it did the dog had odor available.*

Many of non-dog handlers have also expressed their disdain for poor K9 Teams, stating that the only reason the dogs are alerting is because the handler made them. This happens all the time and needs to stop. We learned it is a scientific fact with "Clever Hans", but the handler didn't realize they were doing the tells.

> *Many handlers will essentially tell their dogs to alert/respond because they are afraid to miss something, an alert is needed/wanted, and while they may not verbally be telling them, their actions are; it happens all the time.*

Don't let the dog fail!

I watch experienced handlers with seasoned dogs white knuckle the leashes as if they are afraid to let the dog do its job. The handler has shown the dog the task, the dog is proficient at the task, but will not relinquish the control of the search to the one member of the team that has the powerful nose. Teach confidence to your dog by displaying confidence in them yourself.

There is also a need to let your dog fail, but must be thought through before you truly fail the dog. I see handlers always striving to help their dogs succeed and it is understandable, but essentially a bad lesson for the dog. You have to let them make mistakes in order to provide a venue to show them a mistake has happened.

There are so many examples I can give you on why preventing your dog from failing teaches the wrong thing. I'll try to sum it up like this. Do you want the dog to learn the test or the material? Learning the material is far more important than learning the test, because the test is just teaching the routine or pattern, the material is teaching the dog to use its brain to problem solve.

Letting them fail and more importantly properly illustrating to the dog what they did was wrong and what right is. The example is explained below when I wanted to place narcotics in a venue for explosive detection.

People and dogs both do better work when they feel challenged. If you're bored or doing routine work that doesn't use even your current level of skill, then the probability is that it's showing up in your performance and your team's performance.

Always challenge yourself and your dog, as long as there is a rhyme or a reason for what you are trying to accomplish. When I was working with an explosive dog, I wanted to see if my dog would alert to narcotics. My trainer asked me why and what would I do if he did?

I wanted to see if the strong odor of narcotics would tempt my dog into alerting for a chance at a reward. Knowing that my dog could in fact alert/respond to the new odor, I prepared an explosive training aid in the same vicinity.

The explosive odor was near enough to the narcotics that the dog had the ability to go to the correct odor for a reward and if it chose to make the wrong choice, I had the ability to make a correction quickly and then show what the right choice should have been. The point is there was a rhyme and reason for this and that was good enough for him.

To push your partner to higher levels, you have to keep a balance of positives and negatives so that he knows what he is doing wrong or right and continually challenge him to improve. I will present an advanced problem for a K9 that I feel is currently advanced for their skill level, yet the dog shows the ability to accomplish the task.

If the K9 does well, I generally go back to a more advanced version of what I was just doing, but not the level the dog showed me they could accomplish. Just because the dog did it once right doesn't mean they can do it consistently or as effective. What the dog did show me was a baseline that I can advance from.

If the dog is showing you the ability to understand the material you are presenting to it, then you must first ensure consistency at a basic level and then consistency under stress. A dog can be taught to sit in minutes on command. While it <u>has</u> the ability to perform this task constantly under stress, it hasn't demonstrated that it <u>can</u>. You the handler have to teach the dog that you not only want them to sit, but not get up, wait until I tell you to move (even if it is a long time from now), then you might or might not get a reward until we are completely done with the task.

I watch handlers attempt to advance a dog faster than it is ready. This is usually done because of personal desire and if stopped can help to prevent future problems. Dogs graduating a basic handler course are thrown into advanced working conditions to which the dog hasn't experienced, simply because an employer has to recoup their expenses. Give the teams a chance to acclimate to their new surroundings and environments, allow the team to conduct training and speak to them about what they feel the dog can and cannot handle.

Personally, I train my dog to accomplish level two before I compete at level one. This gives the dog the confidence to do a more advance problem consistently, so when they are tested at a lower level it seems easy and they usually have a higher performance.

"Leadership is learning by doing, adapting to actual situations. Leaders are constantly learning from their errors and failures."
-Claude Meyer, Swissair

Consistently, we observe that the weakest muscle in the body is the one between the ears. Self-imposed limitations and beliefs hold most people back. (**Leadership Challenge Kouzes/Posner**).

I'd like to finish this section out by saying this. We have talked about and established the two rules of dog training. Essentially everything after that is simply a belief, because we can't ask the dog if it is true or not. Most of what we know about dogs have been illustrated through science and their studies, however, most of these studies don't factor in the handler or human.

Trainers and training in the K9 Industry tend to take personal belief foremost and don't truly listen to what they are saying. What I suggest is to take what you are being told and put it in the format of a human. If it doesn't sound right in human, it usually isn't right in K9 either.

Humans need to segregate and discriminate we have and will continue to do so, I guess you can say it is just human nature. I feel that the rest of the worlds creatures don't and this causes ripples in our working dogs. We humans think that only this breed, sex, reward, training method or whatever else is "The Way", but if you said that only this race, gender, payment, religious belief is "The Way", that wouldn't make sense now would it? Step away from what you are being told and decide if it is fact or belief.

Patrick Currey

ELEVEN

Importance of Initiate Incremental Steps And Small Wins

Why incremental steps? Why small wins if we're talking about challenging the process, why not start big? Your dog can certainly do this work it just needs to be communicated to them that you want to have them use their nose on command to find what you are looking for.

Quality is where training should be, never Quantity, one good training session is much better than several average problems.

The first thing that must be realized in a problem is that you as a handler "ARE THE PROBLEM". This is very hard for every handler I have ever worked with to admit, even if deep down they know that it is true, they just don't want to believe it. Especially for those that have been around for a few years and are expected to know better, won't admit they are the problem out of pride.

If you are in a position that you're having a problem with your partner, you must swallow all that pride and look to yourself for the answers. I worked with a handler that wanted to do well with his partner, but he was given bad instruction from the beginning which made it all the more difficult to bring to light what needed to be done to fix the problems at hand.

Once the handler realized that what they were causing the problems with the dog, the handler was then able to focus on not making the same mistakes repeatedly and the dog got better.

Many handlers I work with, I tend to be at least the third trainer. It is tougher as the third trainer to help the handler to see the problems, because I am now dealing with "what my last trainer said" or "my last trainer told me never to".

I like to use video to help a handler see the flaws that they don't feel are causing the problems. Even after I have sat and reviewed tapes with handlers, pointed obvious errors out to them, and they still didn't want to admit it was them, or blame someone or something else.

This problem might even result from your first teacher. For example, if you were taught that the color blue was red, in turn you taught others blue is red, my stepping in and telling you that blue is blue and red is red won't make you believe me.

Either way you want to look at this, if you train incorrectly it is still wrong no matter how many times you do or have done it. Quality training will always win the war.

Two green working dogs enter a quality based training program and a third enters a quantity based program. The two quality K9 are taught 15 different odors over a three week training session, the quantity K9 was still on one odor. The quality K9 were also training their dogs in practical working environments, the quantity K9 was still running can lines.

Why Do Small Wins Work?

Once you realize what the problems are within yourself, you can start the process to becoming a productive team. The problem didn't just manifest itself overnight, while there is the possibility for this to occur, it more than likely developed in small increments that you just weren't looking at. Since the problem developed itself in small steps, you must take the same route to fix them.

Never rush a fix, and never believe in the "quick fix" as that is just like taking the top off a weed, it's gone for a while, but comes back stronger. Find the root of the problem and you will fix what is wrong and build a strong foundation, this is also a very good example of why quality will always win over quantity training.

It is, however, absolutely essential to take risks. Don't be afraid to make mistakes, unless you continually make the same mistake over and over again, it important mistakes and failure are to success.

"Success does not breed success. It breeds failure. It is failure which breeds success."

Nothing is ever done perfectly the first time someone tries it—not in sports, not in games, not in school, and most certainly not in dog training. The point isn't to promote failure for failure's sake. I don't advocate for a moment that failure ought to be the objective of any endeavor. Instead, advocate learning. Leaders don't look for someone to blame when mistakes are made. Instead, they ask "What can be learned from the experience?" (Leadership Challenge Kouzes/Posner).

This is the basis for all learning as a handler. You will go up and down in your working abilities, have many bad training days especially if you're working on a specific problem. If you realize what you have done wrong, work to fix those problems, then your failure breeds success. This is a dance that will require many toes to be stepped on to make it look pretty. I tell people all the time that they will learn more from watching a bad handler work, than a good handler. Because a good handler looks pretty when they work, and you can certainly see the flaws of a bad handler.

The only way that a dog can learn is by doing things they've never done before. Those who do only what they already know how to do never learn anything new. Promoting learning requires you showing your dog just what you want from them and don't allow the option to make the wrong decision.

When I teach a dog to walk up stairs, I stand in a position that the dog only has one direction to go and that is up. If there is enough slack in the leash, the dog can make the wrong choice and a learned behavior is formed.

If you keep a tight leash and only give them one choice, which is the right choice they will take that first step. Use your tone to encourage them to advance like you would an athlete not a baby, make it firm and encouraging. The K9 is always telling you a story. Take the time to see what they are telling you and then use their strengths and weaknesses against them.

One of my dogs didn't like stairs, when I found this out, I saw it as their weakness. That dog also valued the tug so much that it was willing to do anything for it; now its strength is also its weakness and its weakness is now my strength. I used the tug to play a game with the dog and slowly got the dog to forget the stairs because it wanted the tug.

TWELVE

Experiment And Learn From Mistakes

Leaders are experimenters: they experiment with new approaches to all problems. A major leadership task involves identifying and removing self-imposed constraints and personal beliefs that block innovation and creativity. Mathematically a helicopter can't fly, but we see that the inventor didn't listen to others beliefs; he innovated and proved they could fly.

I always say that if you have a rhyme and a reason for training you will succeed. I am frequently asked how long the dogs effectively work.

That is a question that technically has no answer; however, you can and should push your partner to work longer and longer with positive results. This will build endurance and make them realize that even when their tired, if they work a little harder they will find what their looking for and get their reward.

One must periodically set their partner up for failure. Remembering that failure equals success and that when you do this you must give the failure a success.

Little things like placing training aids out so that odor can't help but hit your dog in the face. Just stand near it not saying anything and see what they do. I have watched veteran dogs walk past odor, simply because they weren't told to search, even though they knew the odor was there.

Now remember that this failure needs to equal success, so when your partner puts his nose on the odor and walks away, you must make them feel stupid for walking away, while encouraging them to go back and give the desired alert. "Where are you going?" (in a questioning voice), "Get back here." (point to source that you have now hurried over to), "What do you have there?" (by this time, you should see the look of embarrassment in your dog's face).

When he realizes the error and gives the desired response, you must give a hardy praise, both physical and verbal with the reward. Do this again at a different time during the same day. You should see a change, as they don't want to fail the same way twice. In the event they do, utilize the same method to get them on source.

Moral of this story: Always keep them guessing!

One of the most important items to look out for as the pack leader is that one must continually encourage your partner to venture out on their own, as you can't see what they smell. They look to you for everything, to keep them safe and happy, thus you must do this in a non-verbal way. We know tone of voice is the most important venue we have, so it's not what you say, but how you say it!
Don't be afraid to give a calm good job, every-so-often or a pat on the back as they are busting their butt to search for you. You will find a warm thank-you or good-job goes a long way for your partners desire to continue to find the odor, get their reward, and most importantly PLEASE YOU!

"You can never step in the same river twice, because the water is always flowing."

Break Mindsets

The worst thing that you can do with a K-9 is set a pattern. Patterns can be formed in EVERYTHING we do, utilizing the same training site, same person planting, moving too fast, training days different from work days (Note: you should have a separate training day, however, you should look to vary this up as much as possible. Nights, days, uniforms, civilian clothing, different teams, the list goes on.)

Utilizing the same training odors for too long, moving too fast, to slow, keying your partner to the odor, talking, not talking, talking when there is odor, talking until there is odor. This list also goes on. While you can't ever be perfect, you should ALWAYS keep this in the front of your head each and every time you work or train your dog.

First, don't be afraid to look outside the box for a solution to a problem. I worked with a handler whose partner became afraid of loud vehicles, as well as a few leadership issues as the handler. The inexperience of the handler, lead him to believe that soothing the behavior (reinforcing the behavior.), then rushing the K-9 back into the feared environment, making it worse. The handler even thought it was a good idea to place odor around the fear, so now the poor K-9 associated the odor and the fear as one.

Instead of utilizing the reward to encourage the K-9 near the object, we backed-off and played ball near the environment. This way, if the problem began to increase, the K-9 wouldn't associate the reward and the fear, and no major ground is lost. Once we showed the K-9 that the area could be fun, and that loud noises were part of life, the K-9 began to relax and we were able to take small steps into larger ones, until we leaped back into a normal work routine. (Note: the loud noise wasn't a one time learning incident. The handlers micro-management as a leader, combined with many little unnoticed warnings built up to this becoming a problem).

Always remember how important it is to take small steps every inch of the way. One doesn't become a black-belt overnight; this is a long disciplinary process that takes years of hard work to develop the skills needed.

Give the dog choices

Give your dog a choice about being part of what's happening, and they're much more likely to be committed. All dog training is a "long con", you want the dog to believe they are doing what they want, while all along you are shaping them to do it in the first place.

If your partner wants to search an area, give them a chance to check it out, as we know by now that we can't see odor and have no idea what they smell. This will satisfy any curiosity your K9 may have in that area. Like if I told you that I have a very important life-threatening item to tell you, but won't be able to tell you until the end of the day.

What will you be thinking about all day, and will you be able to concentrate on your job, or be the least bit productive?

I was told by my First Sergeant it only takes one "Awe Crap" to wipe away ten "Atta Boy's". Learn to end training on a good note or a success. Run don't walk away and make the dog feel like they just won the Super Bowl, the next time you run the problem give them every opportunity to succeed to engrain the positive training.

Admit Your Mistakes

Know that you are always the cause of the problem. 99% of the time it is the Handlers fault, the other 1% of the time it is the handlers fault. You failed to lead or communicate at the right moment, learn when and where your problem is and don't keep making the same mistake.

THIRTEEN

Creating A Climate of Trust

Trusting your dog pays off. "I never knew that a lack of trust was our problem (at work) until that exercise. I knew that things weren't going well, but I never really could quite understand why we couldn't work well together. After that experience, things fell into place." (Leadership Challenge Kouzes/Posner).

If I asked a handler if they trusted their dog, the answer would most certainly be yes, however if you put them to the test you will find that most don't truly trust. I feel this is most evident when you watch a handler work their dog on-leash, as they are very controlling of the movements and won't give any slack for the dog to do its job.

You will go through different levels of trust throughout your careers together. Starting in training, trust is different than after your first year. But to truly trust your partner, you have to open your mind and let them do what you have spent so much time training them to do. I have a cartoon of a manager talking to an employee that say's it best: "Why aren't you working?" "I didn't see you coming!" This will happen to your partner if you're not careful with your actions. They will wait for you to work, let you make all the decisions even when they know you're wrong, they will opt for your input only.

I set up training problem one day with two pounds of Marijuana about five feet high in the middle of a warehouse rack. I knew that the wind direction was bringing the odor straight into the dog, with the intent of having the dog drag the handler straight to the source, but to the contrary, the handler continued to pull the dog back controlling it from doing what it was supposed to do in the first place, or what I call MICROMANAGING the dog. By the time the dog got to the source, it had lost the drive walked past the training aid, thus upsetting the handler.

The fault lies in the handler as they created the same situation I explained controlled the dog to the point that it didn't work, because the boss didn't give them the freedom to do their job. You have to set yourself up to trust your dog when they are right and when you think they are wrong. I can't tell you how many handlers have made their dog sit on a fake piece of dynamite, which the dog sniffed and walked away.

To trust your partner, you must be willing to eat crow if need be. Don't put your pride ahead of your partners trust. Make the call, if it comes out bad, work on it in training. To make a call just for the sake of making one, is not trust, and your partner knows it. Take the incident in Florida where the explosive dog alerted on a car, with the whole world watching. Do you really think this was a true K-9 alert, or was the training not at a level to handle the situation? I would estimate that over 90% of the handlers in the world would succumb to this pressure, because if you clear a vehicle and it goes boom. The world is looking at you for answers, and it is easier to just fall into that residual odor story and be done with it.

Learn to Trust

It is important to know where your training aids are to know all the little alerts, which doesn't make it any easier the first time blind problems are run. You may have doubt, but you need to learn to not show it to your dog. I encourage handlers to run 80-90% of their training as known hides, to include tracks.

You need to know when your dog isn't working, isn't searching for you, isn't on task, isn't at source and also when they are searching, on task and at source. Both are important tools for you as a handler to learn from. If you are running blind all the time, you won't know the important times to reward or correct your dog.

This doesn't mean that you need to always know where stuff is. As the trainer, it is my job to know where source is and hopefully correctly guess where odor is traveling. This way I can teach you along the way and step in when you are falling.

Focus On Gains, Not Losses

During a very difficult track laid for one of my h continually struggled with tracking (him not the dog), the dog found me and other than a rocky first 15 seconds, the dog otherwise did a phenomenal track. Unfortunately the handler was not happy with the results. I asked him what the issue was and he stated the dog started out making mistakes and blah, blah, blah. The handler was upset at something that was about one percent of the track and didn't recognize how difficult of a track and how successful the dog was and chose to focus on the bad not the good. While I agree if it were a real world scenario the dog would have…., the point is, it was training and making mistakes in training helps prevent mistakes in the real world. Either way the handler didn't take the opportunity to reward the dog for an otherwise awesome track.

So, what messages to you think the dog got? Most humans leave their jobs because of bad bosses. Your dog is stuck with you and doesn't have the ability to leave, so make it a good working environment.

The handler acts as a coach and an educator, helping the dog to learn and develop their skills, and providing the institutional supports required for ongoing, experiential learning and maturation. In the final analysis, what the handlers are doing is turning their constituents into leaders themselves.

The point of teaching is so that the student can become the master. Your job as a handler is to teach the material, not the test. Once your dog understands what you want it to do, you must give it room to work and not constantly look over their shoulders telling them how to do a job in which you can't even fathom. Trust yourself, Trust your training and Trust your dog and you will become a great team.

You have to let your dog make choices of their own as this is what this job is all about. You teach your dog to attack humans, then expect them to choose not to attack humans like family, friend or neighbors

.Ve also want our dog to make choices in detection such as sniffing in the garbage can and choosing to not eat the trash or choose to sit and stay because what you are looking for is in it.

The only way your dog will learn to choose right from wrong, is if you show it what right is and why wrong is wrong. To a dog this means you have to keep a balance, give positive and negative reinforcement and be timely in doing it. You have to build their confidence that if they make the right choice they will get a reward worth the decision, if not they will let their leader down.

A dog can't be effective and can't make a difference unless they have a choice. If your dog has no freedom of choice and can only act in ways which you tell or allow it, then how can it respond when it has to make the right choice to please you or the wrong choice to disobey and do what you have taught it to do? Your dog will have to ask you" what to do-even if they think they know what needs to be done and feel they could do it!

During training with a very seasoned handler, I watched him let his dog work odor, then walk away from it only to go back to the very same odor and correct it for not sitting. The dog should have never been allowed to leave the source if it was wrong and the handler knowingly allowed it to make the wrong choice and engrained the behavior that it is okay to leave odor.

Dogs will always be dogs, there sense of smell is why they are working for you, but when they want to smell something strange, and we pull them away...

Many of times this is needed, such as when my Golden Retriever would drag me across a room to eat a kibble of food, but that was found first by providing them with a choice to fail in which the dog
 saw that behavior the next time I was able to nip it in final result.

Simply enough, you have to provide choice for your dog during a training environment which is controlled by a competent trainer that can coach you through these problems, as issues like this come from experience of failing to succeed.

The Practice of Problem Solving

If you don't allow your dog the freedom to put its talents to good use, they'll wind up frustrated.

Give your dog the opportunity to work on its own first and allow them to problem solve in training, we do this in a first pass but forget once a detailed search has begun to allow them some room when they ask for it.

You have to design each training problem to teach the dog more than just finding odor, you have to ensure the problem is advanced enough for them to learn a new skill each time and back off when your dog starts to learn. This isn't something you do in the beginning of training; it is an advanced skill that will be continuous throughout the rest of your training.

Backing off isn't as easy as it sounds, since we begin training micromanaging our dog, then have to learn to trust them. Your new role is to make sure that the dog is put in a position to learn and not let them fail. Putting them in a venue to make mistakes is different than failing, and you need to know when to be constantly involved and interacted with your dog, providing guidance, support, and feedback as they move along. Simply waiting for them to figure a problem out and encourage them to come up with solutions instead of finding answers for them, you will get your dog to be more involved and committed.

Building confidence provides a way for your dog to learn and grow. If you don't allow them the opportunity to build confidence in you as a leader and them as a dog you are never going to get optimal performance as a team.

As a handler it is your job to ensure your dog feels confident that it can adequately cope with events, situations, and people the confront puts putting them in a position to exercise leadership. I find that dogs either have huge stress or no stress in their lives. It is your job as a leader to ensure they understand stress is inevitable so learn to deal with it.

Without sufficient self-confidence, your dog will lack the ability for taking on tough challenges. The lack of self-confidence manifests itself in feelings of helplessness, powerlessness, and crippling self-doubt.

Building self-confidence is building your dog's inner strength associate stress as something they can deal with.

This happens when your dog is working odor, but it is bouncing around so much that it can't properly bracket to source, then begins to get frustrated while the handler stands and watches without helping. Something simple like guiding the dog towards the right path will get them properly back on track, and usually working to source.

FOURTEEN

Leaders are Coaches

As your training progresses you must actively seek out ways to increase choice. This is done by providing greater decision-making authority and responsibility with daily and weekly training. Your daily training is far more important than weekly training as you are actually working and can easily promote a short work day for your dog by not getting them out of the vehicle and working them.

Training problems need to be working problems to the dog. I remember a handler I worked with whose dog worked on training days equally as good as mine, however the handler told me the dog didn't work half as good during the real thing. This is because they train differently than they work.

I know that my daily training was no different than my weekly training and I gave my dog the impression that work is work, so always give it your best effort. Use training days for your coach to identify areas you need improvement as a team and give you guidance to increase your performance level.

You as a handler must push yourself to conduct quality daily training which will give the dog the illusion to perform no matter what day it is. When it comes to training there are only **EXCUSES** or **REASONS**, so when you are telling me why you didn't conduct training first ask yourself if you are giving an excuse or reason. You can always do something to promote a solid work ethic even in play you can build on the dog's skills, but if they are always lying around waiting to work they aren't building strengths.

During weekly training I am a coach rather than a trainer. To me "Trainer" is the word associated with the job, and generally the mindset of the person conducting it.

Coaching is different from training, as a coach teaches then lets the pupil execute in a manner they have been taught, while making necessary changes as the situation dictates.

A trainer should be just like a football coach. The handler is the quarterback that has to lead the team (the K9) to execute the plays fundamentally. The coach also has to teach teaches different aspects of those plays and how to read defenses, and know that once the ball is snapped it is the quarterback (handler) utilizing the learned skill alone making a decision. After the play, the coach gives constructive criticism to point out pluses and minuses improve the skills for the future, and most importantly have the bigger picture in mind.

During your career as a canine officer, you need to become the coach and strive for the big game. Fortunately for you, you only have to focus on coaching one player and not the entire team, as a trainer would.

Accentuate the Positives

"Never underrate the importance of visibly appreciating others and their efforts". - Joan Nicolo, Computing Resources, Inc.

To succeed with your dog is to recognize that it is about acknowledging good results and reinforcing positive performance.

I spoke before about work ethic and how it is needed for your dog to understand the job it is doing. In the beginning the work is easy and the task is fun; however when it stops being fun is where you need to learn the balance to keep it a game worth playing. To a working dog, this would mean that you need to show the dog that when they are right you will follow, when you see them going in the wrong direction you refocus them until they are back on track, allowing them to take charge of the search when they are focused again.

This would also mean that you have to reward according to the task, while remembering that rewards take many forms and not just the final reward.

Talk to your dog while you're working, changing your tone of voice, give them a good dog, good job, that's the way, a rub, stop for a few to give them some love. On the same note, when they are working like they don't care you need to let them know with voice tone and your actions.

I was working with a team that worked very well together, and generally only needed minor coaching. This particular day, the dog was messing around and not really focusing on the task, it dragged the handler to the vehicle where the training aid was located, then just stopped caring. The handler continued to let the behavior weaken until the dog walked away. I directed them to research the area with a detailed search, and the dog responded to the training aid, and of course the handler reached in and gave the dog its usual reward, thus rewarding the dog for a low work ethic.

The action was rewarded equally each time, and the dog didn't know the difference between getting paid for hard work or sloppy work. You must always reward you're dog in some form or fashion, but the reward must reflect the deed, to include going hysterical when they bust tail to find an aid. If a human gets paid the same for good performance or poor performance inevitably it will settle with poor performance. However, if you continually strive for good performance a strong work ethic can be formed.

Your dog needs to know if they're making progress toward the goal or simply marking time. A dog needs motivation to increase its productivity on a task increases only when they have a challenging goal and receive feedback on their progress.

In between working one area to the next, I give my dog verbal praise to let them know I am happy with their performance. If they are becoming sluggish I may pick up my tone and pace to show them how I want them to work, but quickly find a way to reward them for the effort.

Eliminate the Negative

It's human nature: when we're being watched by a person who is looking for our faults, we act very differently than we do in a supportive environment in which there's an opportunity to be rewarded for special achievements.

You need to train like you work and work like you train, then rely on yourself, your training and your equipment. If you have studied the material and not the test you can do any work with confidence.

If you are properly training your dog, you won't need to worry about an upcoming certification. All a certification is, is a glimpse at the K9 Teams ability. Certification simply illustrates that the K9 Team passed the basic standards performed on the day observed. It doesn't indicate reliability or effective K9 Teams.

If you are properly training your dog, certification should just be another training day for you. While I don't discourage training here and there to ensure you team can properly perform the guidelines of the certification, strictly working on the certification standards every day weeks prior to certification shouldn't be part of your routine.

Learning to understand and see things from your dog's perspective is paramount to understanding and making this training work. You should end your day asking, "How would my partner rate my performance today? Could I have done anything better?"

FIFTEEN

Being Successful in Training Produces Results

Throughout the start of my career, I have always been the youngest handler. I have had the worst of leaders to work for in what would be called a hostile work environment. My advice to handlers of all levels in their career would be to understand that this is the one job that you will have total control over. No matter who coaches you along the way, you will be the one that makes a great canine or a marginal canine as you are the leader.

You can chose to let the setbacks of the job bring you down, or take a positive approach and never let it get to how you train your partner. I could give you example after example of how others continually attempted to bring me down, but never did I let my partner see it in our work.

Once you are done with training problems put your dog up and go watch. You will find by watching other teams work, you can see mistakes you made, alerts you missed or reassure you are reading your dog properly. It took me awhile to realize the little alerts my dog was sending, I did this by watching others run training after I did.

The next time you see that small alert encourage it and see what they do and know it may take some encouragement for them to show a final result, but it is the start of the positives.

Look at a failure with a positive eye. Failure doesn't equal failure if you find a way to make it a success. It may not always be possible, but if you dwell on the negatives for too long, it will show in your canine's performance.

I can guarantee you a few things in this business. Your dog will always prove you wrong, for every upside there is a downside, and trusting your dog is a two-way street.

To achieve greatness in this business, you must always be the leader, and you alone have the power to choose what kind of leader you will be. Every leader has bad times in their life, but great leaders move past them and learn from their mistakes, so keep a positive attitude while training.

SIXTEEN

The Start Of Detection Training

Scent association is the basic introduction of the odor you are teaching the dog to find. Dogs know how to smell, but we have to train them that a certain scent will get them a reward. How to do this takes many different forms, as Customs utilizes retrieves, ATF "can lines" and the military uses boxes, since "Big Brother" knows all, even they can't decide what is the best way to scent associate a dog.

K9 Operations feels that the most productive for all involved to scent associate is retrieving for tug reward and cans for food. The retrieving method is fun for the canine as they are playing a constant game. The box or can line can become repetitiously boring for both the dog and the handler, so remember this is a game, and when games stop being fun we lose interest in them.

When introducing odor to the canine, you must use the purest form available. This can be done by utilizing pseudo odors that will not harm the canine if ingested. Pseudo odors are a valuable tool that can replace real odors in situations that could be harmful for the real substance. Pseudo training materials will be covered in a further chapter of the manual.

Pure odor is necessary to ensure that the canine is getting the proper scent picture painted. To explain this further, we will place a color with each odor and then break it down a little further as the canine sees it.

<u>Narcotics</u>

Green = Marijuana   **Brown** = Hashish

Blue = Cocaine   **Red** = Heroine

Yellow = Ecstasy   **Purple** = Methamphetamines

Explosives

Green = RDX   **Red** = PETN

Blue = TNT   **Orange** = Acid Salts

Human Scent

Tan = Human   **Brown** = Cadaver

Black = All other odors

Bugs

Burgundy = bugs

Painting a scent picture is very simple with a canine that values the reward. What needs to be considered when introducing odor, is that the canine sense of smell will pick-up all of the odors that are with the smell, thus expand on the overall scent picture and can cause confusion with what odor we are imprinting. For example, a tennis ball has an odor of its own, then if you add green to the picture what exact odor are you trying to introduce, the tennis ball, green or a combination of both. This will always become a common issue on a much larger scale, but if you can eliminate as many of the conflicting odors from the start the better chances of having problems in the future.

We will address conflicting odors and how to take them out of the scent picture in a later chapter.

Tug, ball or food type rewards are utilized by all handlers at K9 Operations. I personally prefer a tug as there is far more to a reward than the object itself. Ball rewards become less tactile rewards from handlers, as most handlers toss a ball and let the canine play.

Food is a great motivation reward and the stomach is a hard competitor to any pray kill drive of a tug reward, but it is harder to reinforce behaviors with food, as it can become sloppy during training so be careful to pick up any food not eaten by the dog.

Tugging requires activity from the handler, and while this won't matter much in the beginning of the training, it will when you get a few years into the dog and they stop working for the reward.

My goal with any dog is to make the reward so valuable that they will do anything to get it. I associate it with being like "crack". Working dogs are selected with drive and motivation for one of the selected rewards, but the most important reward the dog can get is the interaction with the handler.

Last, the reward has to equal the value of the task. Often I ask if you go to work on day one, work 100% and get paid $100 for eight hours of work. Day two, you work 75% and get paid $100 for seven hours of work. How will you work on day three?

This is most important to consider when paying the dog. If they get the same reward every time the reward can lose its value. The reward has to be according to the job performed, good, bad or great you should have a variation to all rewards.

The Selection Process

The K9 selected to become your partner have been chosen from a reputable facility that specializes in working breeds. This person is considered a vendor and has either raised the K9 from their own breeding stock, or purchased the K9 from an overseas contact. Some K9 may have also been selected from other working programs, such as Paws with a Cause, Leader Dogs for the Blind or even a rescue group, or found in a shelter.

Overseas K9 have a very impressive sound to them. For example: German Shepherd Dog from Germany or Czechoslovakia may sound like it is a top of the line subject for any program. The truth of the matter is this; any dog coming from anywhere overseas is considered a reject from their programs. I spent many years working with and befriending many European breeders who stated that they would only let rejects from their program leave the country.

This is not to say that the K9 isn't top of the line, as the breeding is the same and it still has the same parents as the "Top of the Line" dogs staying in their programs. This simply means that in their minds the dog is not up to par.

These dogs are just as good as any other K9 in the program, and will work just as good as any other dog.

My advice over the years from handlers going through the academy is to leave the bias beliefs at home, and look for the dog that is the best, not what you want or like, DRIVE, DRIVE, DRIVE. To many times, I see handlers going for a look, breed, sex or personal preferences, when the most important thing is the canine working, not the breed or looks.

One of the most commonly asked questions is what is the best breed or sex for working dogs? My answer is simply the one that works. Too many people get pig-headed about "The Ultimate Breed". The best K9 for working is the one that fits with your personality and traits. Some breeds are better for first-time handlers and others should be left for experienced handlers. This is not to say that it can't be done, just that experience always helps in this art.

All K9 in this program are carefully selected for their drives. Some meet every criteria, and some meet the major categories when being tested, but every dog can pass or fail a program with only one problem, YOU!!!!

I have selected many potential dogs for the United States Customs K9 Service (Now Customs and Border Protection), during my tenure, and one dog I will always remember more than the others.

I found this Black Lab in an Ohio shelter. The dog took the towel out of my pocket as soon as he was partially out of his cage, and never gave it back. He had no name, so I called him "Bates" after Norman Bates from the movie Psycho, as this dog was nuts for a towel.

I flew with him to Virginia, and he flew through the re-testing process, as several of the instructors commented to me about his drive and need for the reward.

Two months later, Bates failed out of the program during training. I couldn't believe that such an awesome prospect would not make it. Just like human's dogs to have their breaking points, and when I inquired about how a dog like this could fail I was told that the dog just didn't want to work for a bad boss, meaning the handler.

If you were to break the selection process down in a scale form from 1 through 10, with a 10 being the highest, and not letting a dog into the program that isn't above a 7 (70%), I would guess that most dogs test around a 7.5 to 8.5, and the handler is the deciding factor of the dog making it through the program.

All dogs have issues and all handlers have issues. Our job is to match you with the prospects that fit to your personalities and to coach you to work to the dog's needs. If you have a K9 that was selected for you, or you get a choice of dogs to choose from just remember; leave the bias reasons out of the selecting process.

Starting-up

The design of a retrieving exercise is to introduce the odor to the canine by scent association, or playing a big retrieving game with huge odor associated with the reward. This type of exercise is a necessary foundation to introduce the desired odor, and with a strong foundation, we can build the highest towers from. The canine has been chosen for its high retrieve drive, as this is not designed to teach a canine to retrieve, but play = odor = fun for the canine.

It is imperative that odor = fun always or the canine can and will lose the motivation for this work.

Open Area Basic Retrieve

All of these exercises are conducted with a scented reward, which has the odor attached to it. It is important that the canine is in the highest level of excitement to retrieve the article, as this is the process of laying down the detection foundation. The handler will need to play a huge role in getting the canine excited, by teasing the canine with the reward, but not overly excited to scare or make the canine feel as they will be hit.

It is best to start in a low cut open field, preferably fenced in with minimal distractions. Initially the canine will be retrieving by sight, and the reward will have been saturated with the strongest odor.

At the peak of the canines excitement, throw the reward for the canine to chase down and find easily with a verbal command of "FIND IT", once the canine has the reward, a joyous verbal praise followed by a physical game of tug-o-war with be conducted. Remember you're leadership skills, as this is an important time to start working on them. You're partner doesn't understand anything but a fun game is being played at this point, so you need to make this fun or they will soon lose the drive for this work.

Letting the dog have the reward to long can be as hazardous to this process as showing no emotion during the game. You want to get the canine to understand that the towel equals the odor, so when a good game has been played you will look to take the reward back. If the canine drops the reward at any point in the game, you should excitedly take the reward and give it a believable fake throw. Understand that this will be very hard for both you and especially the canine, as you are both uncoordinated, so continue to make an honest effort to improve after each exercise.

You will be given pointers along the way to make the game fun for your particular dog during the exercise, so always keep an ear out for the instructor's commands.

This game will continue for a few trials, and then progress into buildings and vehicles. The building basic retrieve is helpful in introducing this type environment the canine will be searching in a more confined and confused location. The process is started at the door of the building, with the towel being thrown into the open door and the K9 given the command to "find it" while letting go of the collar.

Vehicle exercises will be conducted throwing the towel into the open door of the vehicle the same process as the building, then continued to be conducted in the trunk and under the vehicle exterior.

This is all new to a K9, and they might not want to go into an area for the fear of not knowing, so lead them through this by showing them it is safe.

Introduction of Odor

When it comes to the introduction of odor it really doesn't matter to me what way you teach it. I have found controlled retrieves are the most fun for dogs, but when it comes to explosives and bugs the material utilized for training isn't compatible to this way of odor introduction.

Cans or boxes are the typical way to introduce odor and clean paint cans are far more convenient than boxes. Not to mention that you can clean them a lot easier and maintain them longer.

We are simply working off of Pavlov's study and putting it to work with odor instead of using a bell. I start all dogs with the most powerful odor of what I am teaching as well as a large amount of it.

It is a simple judgment issue on my part; if a human can smell it easily than the dog should have no trouble with it. The amount isn't a science, but some people tend to start out with smaller amounts and I feel that if we can make it easier to get the dog understanding what we are teaching then the better.

It is important to keep the imprinted odor to a pure form, so gloves must be worn while placing the material inside the can, as well as the can itself has to stay consistent. The can with the material in it will be called the positive can, the rest are negative cans. The material has to sit in the can for approximately 30 minutes and there will be 4 cans to start lined up in a row.

A tight leash will start out as we are directing the dog to the first can. I start the dog about two steps away from the positive can.

Always ensure that your reward is readily available and plentiful (food rewards). Get the dog stationed in front of the can and take the first step forward while a clear visible to the dog hand gesture from the dogs nose to inside the can.

The dog generally will move with you and stick its nose inside the can. You are going to be in a bent forward position and don't move until you are ready to reward the dog.

Once the dog has had a chance to sniff the can a command of sit is given (assist if necessary) still not moving from your position, say "OK" and stand and reward the dog. It may seem like a harder process at first to stay in the position, but the dog will catch on very quickly and you will have to fix the cues later in the process. It's better to start out with a pure sent picture and I always emphasize that movement, tone and touch are going to be part of the scent picture along with odor. Photos are in the "Reference Section, Lecture Slides".

This process will continue for about 5-10 times. Ensure that the dog's nose is in the can and that the dog is in a sit before you say "OK". The game has to be fun, but short as the dog needs to value your part in the game (praise, physical attention and interactive play from you). The game should leave the dog wanting more game, too much will tire the dog and less rounds can be run. Ideally the dog should have 10-15 minutes between sessions and I try to do at least three sessions each day.

By the end of the first day, the dog should be sitting before you give the command to sit. I call this" beating you to the correction". Even though you are not physically correcting the dog, there is still a form of correction in the command, so once the dog gets to the can, sticks its nose in and sits you don't have to verbally tell it to sit.

You do have to mind your posture as you still want the dog to see you with your hand in or near the can while in a presentation position. Don't move your body till you say "OK". The dog is a patterned animal, they are trying to bracket which patterns that you are looking to teach and the reason for not moving until you say "OK".

Breaking it down science like:

- Conditional Reflex (Teaching the dog)
- Conditional Stimulus (Odor in the can)
- Conditional Response (Sit)
- Unconditional Stimulus (Reward)
- Unconditional Response (Alert) - won't be seen until the dog advances in the next stage of training.

By the second day the dog should understand at minimum to go to the first can, sniff and sit. I reinforce this from the very beginning going back to the steps from the previous day. The faster the dog shows me they got it, the faster we move along.

The next step is to move the positive can to the second position. The dog will likely try to sit on the first can, so timing is important with your leash control. I simply give a gentle tug on the leash with a command of "NO" to the dog, while I am moving to the positive can, "Good" as the dog is leaving the first can on its way to positive can. Follow the same process as the first can (hand in can, don't move, and assist with a sit, "OK", reward).

The dog should get the picture quickly that they have to sniff the first can then to the second. Once they are at about 80% with little to no assistance from the handler we move it to the third then the fourth can.

By the third day, the dog should have a general idea of the odor they are looking for and what they are expected to do when they identify it. If the dog can run the first phase at about 80-90% of limited handler assistance going from position 1 then 2 then 3 then 4, it is time to move on. If not, the steps have to be repeated until they do.

Second phase should be mixed variables to ensure the dog isn't just looking for a pattern from the pattern. I sometimes will put conflicting odors like food, ball, tug or gloves in the negative cans, but it really depends on the dog, this is called "Discriminating Odors". It should be utilized only when the dog understands the game and I go dog to dog when deciding if it is time. If the dog is going after any of the discrimination odors during the process, "No", tug, "Good" and repeat until the positive can. It should decrease after a few rounds, but if it doesn't eliminate the discrimination odors that are conflicting (food/ball) and replace with a more neutral odor like a vial or glove.

Third phase should simply be reinforcement of the behaviors and I generally add more negative cans at this point.

The process can get tedious and boring for both handler and dog, so placing 12 cans in a circle with 4 positive odors at the 12, 3, 6 and 9 o'clock positions and negative cans filling in the rest. I will fill some of the negative cans with conflicting odors, but not all. Ensure that you are continually in front of the dog with your movements and that the dog has its nose in the positive can before you tell it to sit.

Three rounds with the third phase and the dog should have a pretty good understanding of what it is supposed to look for and what isn't on the menu. Once the dog is beating me to the cans I will let it sniff on its own, while I am walking next to the dog. Most important thing is to not let the dog leave the odor at any time.

An assisted sit is important as well as ensuring that you don't square up to the dog or stop moving at any point.

This will be a very quick pattern the dog learns and a very hard one to break later in training. Day three is simply reinforcement of the odor, movements and discrimination odors. I start to give the dog the opportunity to sit unassisted, but only a few seconds until I assist. The reward for an unassisted sit WILL outweigh that of the assisted. Don't assume anything, start each day with the basics and let the dog show you what they know and don't know. I will also move the positive cans around to different positions in the clock and vary it up each pass.

Day four the dog will begin the clock with mixed variables and should just be all about reinforcement of the smell odor sit, reward pattern. By the second or third phase I start to put the odor in cans along the wall and vary the levels from floor to nose level.

The dog already knows to search the cans, so it shouldn't be a big process for them to be along the wall or to search higher than floor level.

Presentation and movement are key from the handler and most important not to let the dog leave odor at any time. Perfect practice makes perfect performance, so the more you do it right the more the dog will understand what you want them to dog.

Day five I will start out like day four, but I will start to move the odor out of the cans and into very easy to search areas along the wall of the room. I will utilize my physical presentation skills as well as verbal skills to get the dog to sniff the areas I want and likely assist the sit for the until the dog beats me to the correction. Three phases should be run and the dog can make a few passes each phase. I tend to put more out of the cans than in, as well as putting cans in the middle of the room to search that after the exterior is completed.

Just remember this is teaching positive reinforcement. The game should be fun and understood by the dog what exactly you want them to do. The more you vary up your skills the harder it will be for the dog to understand what you want them to do. If you do the right thing every time, the dog will quickly follow. Same goes with doing it wrong and that is much harder to move forward with negative behaviors.

The process for introduction of searching a room is the same as with cans. The first area you present should be positive odor, then begins a work ethic. Not every area that you search will have a positive result. It is your mission to coach the dog into believing that you will let them do the job you have taught them. It is also your job to enforce the negative behaviors with a negative from you and reinforce positive behaviors according to the work being done. I have given several examples of this in previous chapters of this book, if you don't know by now what I am referring to you need to read again.

Patrick Currey

SEVENTEEN

Working Principles Of Dog Training
The Dance

I was once accused by one of my managers of utilizing the principal skills from dog training which I was taught by my agency for personal gain. My response was that the service did not corner the market on this subject and that all of dog training is just a theory, based on scientific evidence from Ian Pavlov, B.F. Skinner and others that we have already given examples from in a previous section. They are simply theories because you can't ask the dog for validation.

It should be very clear by now through reading this manual and classroom work how important you and your leadership abilities are in helping you get through this program. You will begin to see the evidence of this once training begins and is why this manual starts with "Leadership".

You as a handler must know and show how to properly perform every exercise before graduating from this program. During each phase of training, a specific pattern or search sequence will be shown and how it is to be accomplished along with coaching of how to improve upon this. This search sequence is known as non-verbal communication, of which your partner understands as "Leadership Style".

As a handler, you must know the techniques and how to perform them as they will be evident in the dog's performance. It will be the job of the coach to explain and demonstrate these procedures properly, and will expect you to perform them correctly during training.

If you fail to perform a specific method or procedure or the coach fails to explain it properly, the K9 will ultimately be engaged improperly and a mistake like this could take hours of additional training to correct. It is imperative that you know how to perform and exercise as a handler before you perform it as a team.

I advise all teams the best time to practice these skills is without the dog for search patterns, or when giving the dog a break for leash control skills (cans are a great way to practice your skills). You as a handler must know the dance steps before you can get your partner to believe in you, so practice them in your spare time, while you are talking on the phone, watching television or while waiting to run a training problem.

Leash control is the hardest and most important skill to learn, as every handler looks like they have two left hands when starting out. You will not be allowed to have your partner off-leash for the first year, with the exception of a designated training need. Every time you take the dog for a break, it is looking for odor of a good place to go to the bathroom. This odor is just as important to the dog as the odors we are trying to teach them, but with one major difference; you can't break the desire for the dog to find a spot to go to the bathroom, but you can break the drive to search for trained odors.

Practice moving with your partner, when, where and how fast they want to move, as this is a dog doing the same behavior you are asking them to do in a controlled environment.

Get use to keeping up with them, gets them use to you being on the other end, and how you move or giving them the slack for the first couple of steps, then reel in the leash like a fishing reel. This will be explained in further detail during a classroom exercise; however it is the most important process to learn for you to be a successful handler.

Practice

We have demonstrated to you that the K9 learns by association, which is emphasized by repetition as a foundation for their learning process, and how each new task is taught.

This process is essential for the K9 to repeat each exercise over and over until the desired level of proficiency is achieved. It is important to understand that while the dog learns through association and practice, doing an exercise properly once is more important than doing several exercises (quality versus quantity).

Any training exercises should be able to be run by a team at any level, but geared to the level of the team running at the time. Dogs become bored just like people, and the exercise has to always be fun, enjoyable as well as challenging for the dog. I have witnessed many K9 that simple get bored with the routine and simple get complacent. Each exercise is designed to teach the team something new. They are not just thrown together, as they are the factor to success. This training is important to expose the K9 to new environments, and perform different tasks, keeping them from becoming bored, or regressing in their training.

Patience, Praise, Correction and Timing

Each one of these categories is a leadership trait, in which you must learn when and how to utilize them. If not done in a timely manner none of them will work effectively and the K9 will become confused and a breakdown in the relationship begins.

Trust me when I tell you that your K9 loses patience long before you ever will. This is very frustrating for each of you to learn each other's languages, and while we can sit and talk about what is happening, the dog can't. This is why it is important for you to keep your cool during training at all times.

Patience is the first skill you must master in this art, for if you lose patience it not only creates confusion, but nothing ever constructive is accomplished when you lose patience.

Praise/Tone is how we get the K9 to understand that the trait they are doing is what we want them to do. The problems handlers face is of timing and becoming mundane with the praise. If you praise the dog for a good trait then praise them equally for a bad trait, what does praise mean to the dog?

Handlers will praise their K9 equally for performing at the top of the game, as they do when they are performing poorly. An example would be a boss giving a bonus to an employee for being top sales and the same bonus to an employee that has the lowest sale. The praise negates itself and will simply mean nothing special to the worker, or even cause them to look for another employer.

Correction is the process of showing the dog right from wrong. Praise the right and correct the wrong, is pretty simple in theory. Overcorrect and the K9 will fear, un under-correct and the K9 will be in charge.

A correction takes on many different forms, simply not praising can be a correction just as a verbal admonition spoken in an unpleasing tone of voice or a quick sharp jerk on the leash is a correction. You must also master the art of correction as it will need to take many forms for you to achieve greatness in this field. Remember my golden rule; "A correction isn't a correction unless it stops the behavior and doesn't have to be physical to correct".

Timing is the key to making any of these disciplines work for you. The K9 must associate the Praise/Tone or Correction with what they did right or wrong, as they cannot mentally connect the action they did as a positive or error if the timing is minutes or even seconds before the act. Simply, a dog that urinates on the floor while you are away will not understand the yelling when you walk in the door, thus causing more confusion and bigger problems in the future.

Never correct for clumsiness or the dog being behind the learning curve. This only slows down the learning process instead of moving forward. They are trying to learn something that isn't natural for them, so don't get frustrated that one dog isn't learning as fast as another.

To put this into perspective in a business sense, these skills determine the work ethic that becomes behavior.

EIGHTEEN

Kennel Sanitation and Safety of the Dog

To ensure the proper care and cleaning procedures are maintained for a safe and healthy environment for your dog, this section will go over proper cleaning procedures of the kennel area, vehicle and home environment. You have a working dog not a pet, if your dog is not healthy it cannot work you do not have a job. It only takes a short amount of time to ensure your dog has a healthy safe environment.

The term kennel environment will mean the area in which the K9 is housed. This environment includes the vehicle, home kennel or temporary kennels.

Each working dog should have their own kennel environment to ensure the safety of the dog, family and general public. The dog must be secured in the kennel at all times when not in direct control of the handler. Only the handler of the dog or trained personnel (adult) should care and maintain the dog and the kennel environment.

While it is a good idea to get the family involved in every aspect of the dog children and other family members should always be supervised when in the presence of the dog. Remember you are responsible for the actions of the dog and it is never a problem, until it is a problem.

A working canine is a very valuable tool which is the responsibility of the individual handler to ensure a safe and healthy environment for everyone. The handler must follow guidelines and regulations by their individual department or agency for safe housing of their working dog. Always remember what the dog is trained to do, as they will be going through many changes physically, mentally and in training. This is a Working Dog, not a Pet!

Regardless if your dog is trained to attack or not, all dogs will bite and can cause serious damage. The kennel, home environment and vehicle may all become areas the dog considers its territory and can become a place the dog protects. As a handler you should be a see very quickly that your dog is stressed and or not comfortable in its kennel environment, but remember this is your partner not your family members they don't have the same relationship that you do.

Kennel Environment

The kennel environment should be kept free of fecal matter and urine at all times. Many working dogs and civilian industry are not kenneled, but rather live at home and handler. Many working dogs are selected based upon traits that don't always make good house dog's. This doesn't mean that you're working dog can't be taught how to be a properly in your home, just that you need to protect your dog from itself.

If possible a kennel environment should be constructed of dog proof material that will prevent it from chewing, absorbing or escaping (such as concrete or other non-porous materials). A raised platform should be in the bedding area of the kennel made of a non-chew material and the dog should also have a water source available at all times. Work vehicles don't require a raised platform; however a nonslip surface should be place to prevent the dog from sliding.

The kennel environment should be well ventilated and climate controlled. The temperature of the kennels should be comfortable for the dog with the idea that they are a working dog and will need to be adjusted to the climate they are to work. To cool or too warm of an environment can cause a severe impact on the working ability of your dog when they are placed in a rapid temperature change.

Vehicle

The vehicle windows should be left down to allow proper ventilation. The air conditioning can be left on to keep the environment at a safe temperature. The windows should never be completely closed and as a good measure all windows should be left in a half position.

The vehicle should also have a kennel environment to prevent the dog from escaping, biting or damaging the vehicle or themselves. A climate warning system is ideal to alert the handler if the temperature is at a dangerous level and at minimum one gallon of fresh potable water should be available. Vehicles shall also be cleaned from debris and sanitized on a regular basis. The K9 shall never ride loose in the vehicle or permitted to hang out the window. Just remember your dog needs to be acclimated to the environment for which they will be working; a dog sitting in the air-conditioned vehicle will have trouble working on a hot summer day.

Cleaning and Sanitation

The cleaning and sanitation of the kennels should be conducted on a daily and weekly basis. The home kennel environment should be maintained on a daily basis to remove any hair, stool or urine present. Stool and urine should be removed upon notice and the area should then be properly cleaned to prevent an unhealthy environment.

The sleeping platform and kennel should be sanitized at minimum once weekly with a disinfectant that will kill 99% of bacteria and once monthly the area should be scrubbed with a safe cleaning solution and rinsed thoroughly. Water bowls should be changed at minimum every other day, cleaned and sanitized and food pans should be cleaned after each use. All food should be kept in a rodent proof container and in an area the dog cannot get into it.

The home environment should also be safe for the dog. Keep the dog out of areas that have just been treated with chemicals such as the yard in the summer and the salted driveway in the winter.

Fecal Matter

Fecal matter should be picked up after the dog has eliminated as it is a good way to learn about your dog. Look for what is a consistent stool as far as color, amount, size and shape. Loose stools can be simply stress or the start of a problem, to include change of color and if you are not familiar with what is normal you won't know what is bad. Also look for worms, foreign objects and blood.

Blood on the stool can be normal; however any blood in the stool should be addressed with a veterinarian.

Urine

Urine can also be telling if you notice a color change, different smell, longer or shorter durations; inform your veterinarian as they may want to see them for a checkup.

Boarding Kennels

The working dog shouldn't be left unattended in the home for any reason and should always be placed in the kennel when not attended to. The handler is encouraged to interact with the dog and family under supervised times such as play or feeding, then the dog should be returned to the kennel.

During times when the handler is not able to care for the dog, such as vacation time the dog should be placed in the care of a qualified adult. This person should know and understand the working dog and how to properly care for their safety and the safety of others and should in no way work the dog unless there are qualified K9 handler. It is ideal that the dog stay in an authorized boarding kennel which is versed in the needs of a working dog, while the handler is on vacation or away for extended periods of time.

Interaction with Other Dogs

Interactions with other dogs can be hazardous to your dog. This does not mean you are to prevent any interaction, just remember it is your working dog and you rely on both its mental and physical health to perform your duties. Your family dog is your pet and your work dog is your partner, you and your family both need to understand this and the interaction between all should be considered.

Dogs communicate with each other very quickly and a fun event can quickly turn into a dangerous fight that can cause serious harm to both dog and human. Interaction with unfamiliar dogs should be prevented at all times or strictly supervised and interaction with the family pets should be monitored.

Working dogs should not be unsupervised in the yard or home and any contact from any human outside of the handler should always be leashed. It only takes a second for a bite to happen and you have a trained dog that can cause serious injury to humans and other animals.

The general care of the working dog should never be assumed. Each handler should be taught proper cleaning, maintenance and general care of their working dog during their initial training. It is your sole responsibility as the handler to ensure the safety of others from your dog and of your dog from others.

Veterinary Care And Vaccinations

The handler must schedule yearly check-ups with their veterinarian as well as continue with current vaccinations. It is important that a working dog stay healthy and receive proper care for any and all injuries. Each handler should be trained for basic medical care of the dog, to include procedures established outlining their responsibilities. It is also recommended a basic K9 first aid kit be in each vehicle at all times.

Patrick Currey

NINETEEN

Grooming and Health Check

A routine health check is part of, but by no means limited to, the grooming and inspection period. During the formal grooming and health check period, take this opportunity to check over each part of the dog's anatomy for signs or symptoms of illness or injury. Inspection, however, is a continuing process, so always be alert for symptoms of illness or injury.

After you have been with your dogs for a while, you know what your dogs should look like and how they should act when healthy and feeling well. You should know what is normal for his dog, how the dog's coat of hair looks, how many bowel movements the dog has each day, and how much the dog eats a day.

When making a daily health check, use your knowledge to detect anything about the dog that is abnormal.

For example, the animal may not have eaten all of his food for a day or two; he may have an area of hair loss and reddened skin somewhere on his body; or he may have a discharge coming from his nose.

If you notice anything abnormal about the appearance or actions of the dog, it must be reported immediately.

Do not attempt to diagnose the illness and apply home remedies; an untrained person can often do more harm than good. Rely on veterinarians who are trained to provide expert medical care for the dog. Veterinarians depend on the officers to detect and report any symptoms of illness or injury. The early detection of any illness or injury is important. If treatment begins early, the dog has a better chance for a rapid and a complete recovery.

Patrick Currey

It is important for handlers to find and continue training with a qualified trainer, one who can provide these elements, to ensure success as a detection team.

Advanced Bed Bug Detection Handler Training

This is a three week comprehensive course providing handlers both classroom and real world experience in how to read and work their assigned K9 in bed bug detection. Handlers must have a K9 certified in bed bug detection to participate in this course, as this is not a green dog training course. This course will cover much more than just handling skills. Teams will be given classroom instruction and testing in the following areas:

- Principles Of Detection Training
- K9 Behavior
- Basic K9 Anatomy ~Ethology~
- Basic K9 First-Aid
- Science Of Training And Learning
- Scent Theory
- K9 Maintenance Training Skills
- Safety And Health Maintenance (Home/Work),
- Drive And Its Importance In Training
- Practical Home To Work Issues
- Training Record Keeping

The handler's time is balanced between classroom and hands-on practical training. The majority of handler skills training will be conducted in real world scenarios in an effort to better prepare handlers for an actual working environment.

All K9 Teams who pass our certification standards will receive a certificate, valid for one year, stating the team is a trained and is proficient to identify the presence of bed bugs.

We also offer a two-day manager's course at no additional cost. This course will illustrate what is required from management to train and maintain a working dog, record-keeping, operating policies and procedures, and the proper and practical uses of a Detector Dog

Team. This course can be taken during any of the handler training courses throughout the year.

K9 Operations provides detection training for a wide variety of detector dog needs for both Law Enforcement and civilians. Full service training is available for Law Enforcement agency working dogs in Narcotics, Explosives Detection, and Tracking.

Police K9 Training

160 Hour Basic Handler Training Course

This is a four week comprehensive course providing handlers both class room and real world experience in how to read and work their assigned K9 in narcotics, explosives, tracking and apprehension training. Handlers must have a K9 certified for narcotics/explosives detection to participate in this course, as this is not a green dog training course. For agencies needing to purchase a full service K9 prior to attending our next course, please contact pat@k9operations.com and I will assist you in finding the right dog for your program.

This course covers much more than just handling skills. The teams will be given classroom instruction and testing in the following areas: Safety and Health maintenance (home/work environments), Drive and Its Importance in Training, Principles of Detection Training, K9 behavior, Basic K9 anatomy, Basic K9 First-Aid, Science of Training and Learning, Scent Theory, K9 Maintenance Training Skills, practical home to work issues, and training record keeping.

This course will give your handler the basic skills needed for certification with their assigned K9 with an approved certification authority.

Maintenance Training

To ensure the best working dog for your agency, the teams need to conduct both daily and weekly maintenance training.

While the handlers will be given the basic skills to work their assigned dog, this doesn't mean they won't develop working obstacles after completing the program. It would be optimal for your working dog teams to conduct maintenance training in a working environment a minimum of eight hours per month.

K9 Operations offers both weekly and bi-weekly maintenance training. I offer group rates for agencies with multiple dogs enrolled.

For agencies needing assistance determining the cost effectiveness of their detection program please submit an email request for a detailed outline to pat@k9operations.com

www.k9operations.com

K9 Operations
6261 Hannan Road
Romulus, MI 48174
PH: (734) 532-2013
FAX: (734) 532-2017

Made in the USA
Lexington, KY
29 May 2014